A Guide to Britain's Indu

CW00351810

A Guide to

BRITAIN'S INDUSTRIAL PAST

Brian Bailey

WHITTET BOOKS

First published 1985
© 1985 by Brian Bailey
Whittet Books Ltd, 113 Westbourne Grove, London W2 4UP
All rights reserved
Design by Paul Minns
British Library Cataloguing in Publication Data

Bailey, Brian
    Guide to Britain's industrial past.
    1. Great Britain—Industries—History
    I. Title
    338'.0941   HC253

    ISBN 0-905483-42-1
    ISBN 0-905483-43-X Pbk

The author and publishers gratefully acknowledge permission to reproduce the
illustrations that appear on the following pages: Beamish North of England Open
Air Museum, p. 85, p. 104, p. 121, p. 158, p. 160, p. 172; British Tourist Authority,
p. 18, p. 32, p. 54, p. 70, p. 72, p. 99, p. 101, p. 109, p. 113, p. 134; Rita Bailey, p. 50,
p. 95, p. 119, p. 126, p. 156, p. 163, p. 165.

Typeset by Inforum Ltd, Portsmouth
Printed and bound in Great Britain by Whitstable Litho

Glossary

Adit
A horizontal entrance to working areas in mines, as opposed to vertical shaft.

Annealing
Process of cooling glass very slowly to prevent stresses which would cause breakage.

Atmospheric engine
A beam engine which relied on atmospheric pressure to complete the working stroke begun by steam pressure. Steam pressure raised one end of the beam, which was then allowed to fall under atmospheric pressure, moving the other end up and down to operate the pump.

Bottle oven
A brick-built kiln for firing pottery, with narrow neck at the top like bottle.

Breastshot
Type of water wheel operated by water falling at middle of wheel rather than on top or flowing underneath.

Buddling
Process of eliminating impurities from metal ore (chiefly lead). Crushed ore was fed with water into a circular stone trough swept by rotating brushes, which removed residue to leave concentrated ore behind.

Caisson
Working chamber used in laying foundations under water (e.g. for river bridges). Also, water-filled chamber for transporting boats or barges.

Calcining
Process of refining ore by burning off impurities.

Chaldron
A measurement of coal. A chaldron wagon is one built to carry a specified volume of coal. The word comes from cauldron.

Coal drop
A type of crane used at docks to lower loaded coal wagons to the holds of ships.

Coke
Substance produced by burning coal to eliminate impurities, and suitable for industrial use where gases could affect processes.

Crucible
Melting pot made of earthenware and used in making steel by fusing carbon with iron under intense heat.

Deckle	Frame with fine wire mesh used in hand paper-making to separate pulp fibres from water.
Donkey wheel	A treadwheel operated by a donkey, usually to raise water from a deep well.
Entablature	Architectural term for the parts of an order above the columns, such as the architrave and cornice.
Fantail	On a windmill, a small sail device so placed to turn the main sails into the wind.
Feldspathic glaze	Glazing medium for pottery, made from felspar and less hazardous to workers than lead glaze.
Flight	In reference to canal locks, a set of locks in which each has its own gates independent of the neighbouring locks.
Fulling stocks	Mechanical device for thickening cloth by pounding the fabric in water and the clay known as 'fuller's earth'.
Funicular railway	Counterbalanced cable railway with cars moving in opposite directions at the same time on steep gradients.
Glass cone	Glass-making workshop of conical shape with furnace in centre.
Gravity incline	Railway track with slight gradient on which wagons are allowed to descend under their own weight (i.e. without use of engine).
Leat	Artificial channel to conduct water to drive mill wheel, etc.
Lehr	Oven in which molten glass is cooled at controlled speed in annealing process.
Norse mill	A water mill, supposedly introduced by Viking settlers, in which the driving wheel is moved on a horizontal plane, i.e. lying flat instead of standing upright.
Ogee	Contrary curves as in S shape. An ogee arch is one in which two ogee curves join at the apex.
Overshot	Type of water wheel driven by water falling on it from above, usually by means of a leat.
Pediment	Triangular or gable-shaped top part of classical building facade above columns.

Pig	Oblong mass of crude metal produced in smelting process. Applied mainly to lead and iron.
Post mill	A windmill of which the upper part, bearing both sails and machinery, is supported on a massive timber post which allows it to revolve according to the wind direction.
Reverberatory furnace	Furnace in which iron was rendered malleable (for wrought-iron products) by circulating air to remove carbon content.
Riven	Slate or stone split or cloven as required, by quarryman.
Rotative beam engine	A steam-powered engine in which the working end of the beam operated a wheel by means of a connecting rod.
Saddleback roof	Used to describe a normal pitched roof where one would not normally expect to see one, e.g. on a church tower.
Skew arch	In a bridge, an arch which is not placed at right angles to the abutment.
Smock mill	A windmill similar to a tower mill in operation, but usually of octagonal shape and weatherboarded, above a base of brick.
Sough	A ditch or shallow canal cut to drain water away from mine or other workings.
Spandrel	The triangular space between the shoulder of an arch and the rectangular framework of the building or bridge.
Staircase	In reference to locks, an arrangement in which the top gate of one lock is also the bottom gate of the next, i.e. a series of interconnected locks, not independent of one another as in a 'flight'.
Staithe	Timber-built wharf for loading coal into ships.
Stamp	A kind of mechanical hammer for crushing ore. Much used in tin-mining, hence 'Cornish stamps'.
Steelyard	A device for weighing loaded wagons, etc., worked by balancing the load on the short arm of a pivoted beam with weights on the long arm.
Tilt hammer	Heavy pivoted hammer used in forging steel, operated by waterwheel.

Tower mill

Windmill of solid construction in which the sail mechanism is housed in a rotating cap at the top of the building.

Transporter bridge

A girder bridge spanning a river at high level to allow the passage of vessels. Cars are carried between the supporting towers by suspension from a track in the girder.

Treadwheel

Large wheel or cylinder operated by man or animal 'walking' inside it to produce motion.

Undershot

Type of water wheel moved by flow of water beneath it.

Voussoirs

The wedge-shaped stones forming an arch.

Water ballast

System of counterbalancing in cliff railways, etc. Water is pumped from a tank in the car at the bottom up to the one at the top, which then descends, raising the bottom car at the same time.

Introduction

The immense amount of public interest generated in recent years in Britain's industrial past has not, on the whole, been reflected in the literature, which has tended to consist either of books for railway enthusiasts or those written by specialists with an engineering background for those who wish for more or less detailed technical explanation of how things work. I believe there are many people, however, who share my interest in the wider aspects of industry, and not just a fascination with engines. This book is for them, and I have carefully avoided the term 'industrial archaeology' in the title. It is, in my view, a serious misnomer for an enthusiasm masquerading as a science. Most books on the subject confine themselves to the period of the Industrial Revolution, as if nothing that happened before the eighteenth century could be called 'industry', and thus the authors betray their fixations with the development of machinery rather than the history of useful labour. Agriculture is the oldest industry on earth, but these 'archaeologists' rarely mention it. They are, as a rule, even less interested in the people who did the work.

This guide draws attention to the important sites and visible innovations of the Industrial Revolution, but it also includes industries whose origins go back to prehistoric times, and reflects some of the changes brought to the rural landscape and to the urban scene by industrial development.

The guide is arranged alphabetically by place name, and all the towns and villages mentioned can be found on the maps at the end of the book. Districts of Greater London are all classified under London. At the head of each article a symbol appears to indicate what branch of industry it is concerned with, and this reappears on the maps, so that a reader with a special interest in mining, for example, can see where the sites connected with mining and quarrying are in any particular area. The symbols used are as follows:

▲	Agriculture, food and fisheries
△	Mining and quarrying
≈	Canals
=	Railways
+	Transport, bridges, etc. (other than canal and rail)
○	Shipping
×	Power
□	Manufacturing industry
☆	Museums, housing and sites of sociological interest

This system can only be fairly arbitrary, of course. The first entry in the book, Abbeydale Industrial Hamlet, could be classified as ×, □ or possibly ▲. But as the place is now run as an industrial museum, I have regarded ☆ as its most helpful classification, and emphasis is similarly placed on the *chief* attraction for visitors throughout the book. In towns and cities where more than one site is included, only one symbol is shown on the maps to avoid overloading them and causing confusion. All wind and watermills are classified as ×, regardless of their purposes, so that they can be identified separately from such things as maltings, agricultural machinery, etc.

The maps also serve to indicate the pattern of industry in Britain. No one will be surprised to find the greatest concentration of industrial monuments in the English Midlands and North, or of agricultural concerns in the south and east. The oldest industries next to agriculture – mining and quarrying – occur north and west of a line drawn between Weymouth and the Wash. This was dictated by geology, a belt of Jurassic limestone separating the old hard rock with its mineral deposits from the chalk and clay of south-eastern England and East Anglia. Practically all subsequent heavy industry has been determined to some degree by this fact, depending as it does on the need for coal, ores and plentiful water supplies.

Many industrial sites – especially manufacturing concerns – are still working, and there is no public access, but in cases where I mention working factories, mills or other buildings still in commercial use or now private dwellings, the chief interest is in the external architecture or its historic significance. I make it clear when the public can visit the *insides* of these places. With such sites, however, as well as museums and other places normally open to the public, I have not given opening times or admission charges because these are subject to change, and it is advisable to enquire locally before making visits.

The vast majority of items or places listed in this volume can be seen by interested visitors at any reasonable time, and I hope that many of the items not usually found in books on 'industrial archaeology' will give readers some balancing insight into the human history of industry as well as its mechanization.

I have included a few brief biographies of some of the engineering giants of the Industrial Revolution. If we only knew who they were, the men who discovered fire and those who invented the wheel and the plough would take pride of place here. Not that they were British, of course (as far as we know); but their contributions to the human condition were greater and more revolutionary than anything that happened in the eighteenth and nineteenth centuries, when new inventions and techniques were often only logical progressions of what had gone before.

Spring, 1985   *Brian Bailey*

Maps

Cradley He
Stourbridg
Arley =
Bromsgro
☆
Newnham Bridge
Worces
HEREFORD
& WORCESTE
Hereford ☆

Gloucest

Nailswor

AVON
Clifton
Bristol
Kelston □ B
Limpley Stok
Stanton Drew
Shipham △
Chapel △ Smitham
Allerton △ Priddy
□ Wookey h
□ Street
Henley
SOMERSET
Ifracombe
Bideford
Bradford-on-Tone
Tiverton □
DORS
DEVON
Axminster
Honiton
□
Sturmin
Mars
Lyme Regis
Sticklepath
Ottery St Mary
Exeter ☆
Seaton
Delabole △
Haytor △
Mary Tavy △ Down
Princetown
Portland
CORNWALL
Morwellham ☆
Carthew △
Calstock =
Saltash =
Camborne
Hayle
Redruth △
Crwennap ☆
Pendeen △
Botallack △
Devoran
Charlestown
Plymouth
Dartmouth
Hallsands ☆

King's Mills □
Moira □
Glenfield ⇌
Leicester ☆ □ Wigston
□ Loughborough
△ Mountsorrel
△ Swithland
LEICS.

Holkham ▲
○ King's Lynn
NORFOLK
× Sutton
+ Norwich
Gt. Yarmouth ☆
Reedham ×

MIDS.
Dudley
Smethwick
☆ Birmingham
Bournville
Brierley Hill
Tardebigge
Stoke Prior
☆ Warwick
□ Hinckley
Foxton ⇌
□ Coventry   NORTHANTS.
△ Barnack
Holme Fen ▲
Pymore ×
Stretham
Earith ▲
Wicken
Soham +
+ Cambridge
Bourn
△ Santon Downham
☆ Bressingham
Lowestoft
Stowmarket
Saxtead
×
Easton ▲
Snape ▲
Woodbridge
SUFFOLK

WARKS.
Harbury
× Stratford-upon-Avon
Blisworth
Stoke ⇌ Roadel
Bruerne   Newport Pagnell
Wolverton
Northampton ☆
CAMBS.
□ Harrold
× Stevington
☆ Stewartby
BEDS.
East
Bergholt ▲
Mistley × ○ Harwich
× Colchester

Lower
Slaughter ×
Cheltenham
GLOS.
Bibury ▲
⇌ Coates
windon =
acock
BUCKS.
Ampthill ☆
Luton □
Pitstone ×
Brill
Tring =
High
Wycombe
Lemsford ×
Digswell =
△
Ware ▲
Gt. Amwell
HERTS.
Thaxted
×
Gt. Bardfield
ESSEX

□ Chipping
Norton
OXON
□ Witney
▲ Great Coxwell
Nettlebed
Rotherfield Greys ⇌
Stoke Row ☆
Mapledurham ×
St Albans ×
Camden ×
Hampstead + |
Paddington =
Kensington ☆
Strand ×
Brentford ⇌
Kew ☆
St Pancras +
Spitalfields =
Tower Bridge
○ London Docks
St Katharines Dock
= Rotherhithe
Holborn |
Westminster +
+ Wallington
GTR.
LONDON
○ Sheerness
Chatham ○
□ Faversham

Gt. Bedwyn ⇌
⇌ Devizes
Trowbridge
WILTS.
□ Wilton
Marlow □
Maidenhead =
☆ Reading
Theale ⇌   Windsor
☆ Cobham
SURREY
× Shalford
× Outwood
KENT
Dover ○
▲ Sissinghurst
× Cranbrook   Hythe ⇌
Wadhurst ☆
Maidstone □

□ Whitchurch
Binsted ☆
× Winchester
HANTS
W. SUSSEX
Henfield ×
☆ Singleton
E. SUSSEX
= Clayton
Battle =
Hastings ☆

Eling ×
Buckler's Hard
☆ Sway
Fareham
□ Portsmouth
Newport □
☆ Carisbrooke
× Shorwell
× Bembridge
△ Swanage
× Eastbourne

MAP A

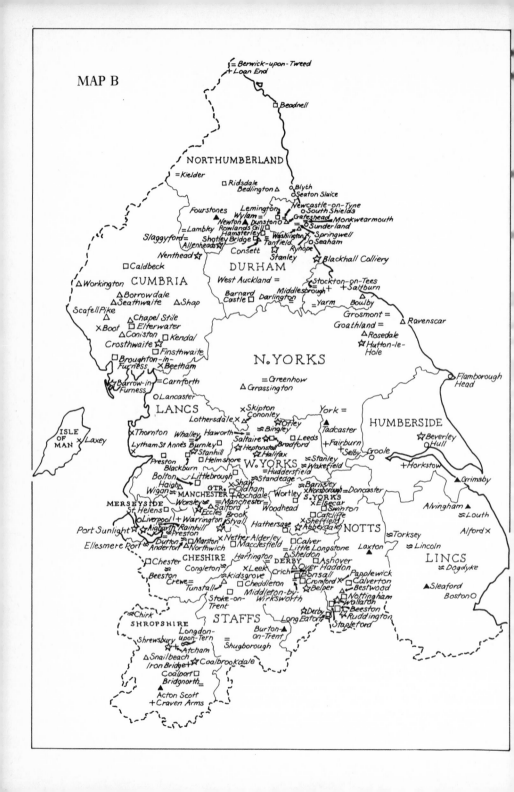

MAP C

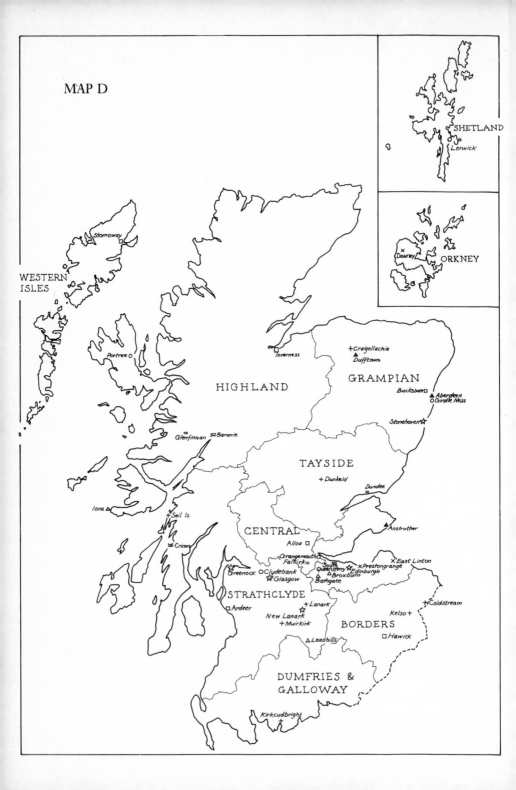

MAP D

SHETLAND

Lerwick

×Dounby ORKNEY

WESTERN
ISLES

Stornoway

Portree ○

HIGHLAND

Inverness

+Craigellachie
▲Dufftown

GRAMPIAN

Bucksburn▲
▲Aberdeen
○Girdle Ness

Stonehaven☆

Glenfinnan≡ ⇟Banarie

Iona △

+Seil Is.

⇟Crinan

TAYSIDE

+Dunkeld

Dundee⇟

▲Anstruther

CENTRAL

Alloa □

Grangemouth○
Falkirk⇟ South
Greenock○Clydebank Queensferry⇟ ×Prestongrange ×East Linton
☆Glasgow ▲Broxburn×Edinburgh
Bathgate

STRATHCLYDE

□Ardeer +Lanark
New Lanark☆
+Muirkirk

△Leadhills

BORDERS

Kelso +
□Hawick

+Coldstream

DUMFRIES &
GALLOWAY

⇟Kirkcudbright

Abbeydale Industrial Hamlet, South Yorkshire ☆ MAP B

This unique industrial museum at the south-western edge of Sheffield was formerly a scythe works, built in the eighteenth century and comprising stone-built mill and ancillary buildings, manager's house and workmen's cottages. Sheffield was already known for its knives by the fourteenth century – Chaucer refers to the miller in *The Canterbury Tales* as carrying a 'Sheffield thwitel' (a large knife). Here at the Abbeydale museum the process of making edge tools can be followed from start to finish. The mill was powered by two waterwheels still *in situ*. One is a breastshot wheel of eighteen foot diameter which drove the tilt hammers; the other drove the blowing cylinders. The factory made scythes and other agricultural edge tools using crucible steel made on the site, and the place continued in production until 1933. Even the crucibles or pots in which the steel was made were produced here, and the pot shop can still be seen. The original complex, with its steel furnace, grinding and boring shops, forges, warehouse and so on, stood in relatively rural surroundings, but is now enveloped by modern housing. Open daily throughout the year. Tel: Sheffield 367731.

Aberdare, Mid-Glamorgan   = MAP C

At Trecynon, a suburb on the north-west side of the town, there is an iron bridge built in 1811 to carry products of the Abernant Ironworks on a tramway from the works to the Glamorgan Canal, and thence to the port at Cardiff.

Aberdeen, Grampian   MAP D

The 'granite city' is the most important of Scotland's east coast fishing ports, and the third largest in Britain. Early morning visitors to the fish market can see the catches – packed in ice at sea and winched ashore to be displayed in boxes – being auctioned from 7.30 a.m. onwards.

Aberdeen, Grampian   + MAP D

The stone Brig o'Balgownie crossing the River Don north of the town was built with its graceful Gothic arch in the fourteenth century by Robert the Bruce. It is referred to by Byron in *Don Juan.*

*Opposite
Tilt Forge at
Abbeydale
Industrial
Hamlet*

Aberystwyth, Dyfed   =   MAP C

The Vale of Rheidol Railway is a narrow-gauge system (1 foot 11½ inches)
running nearly 12 miles from the town to Devil's Bridge. The line was built
in 1902, mainly to convey lead from mines in the valley. It was threatened
with closure after the demise of the lead-workings, but was saved and is
now operated as a tourist service in summer months by British Rail – the
only steam line left in the nationalized network. The locomotives date from
the 1920s.

Acton Scott, Shropshire   ▲   MAP B

At this village off the A49 just south of Church Stretton is the Acton Scott
Working Farm Museum, where nineteenth-century arable farming techniques are demonstrated using Shire horses and steam-powered machinery.
'Obsolete' breeds of animals are also preserved here. The farm is open
every day in the summer months; afternoons only in spring and autumn;
closed in winter. Tel: Marshbrook 306.

Afon Argoed, West Glamorgan   △   MAP C

In the Afon Argoed Country Park, five miles north-east of Port Talbot on
the A4107, is a Miners' Museum, set up by the South Wales Miners
Museum Committee, and a fine exhibition of the conditions and equipment of coal mining in the area. The park itself is on land largely reclaimed
from derelict colliery sites and slag-heaps. The museum is open daily
during the summer months, and weekend afternoons in winter.

Aigburth, Merseyside   ☆   MAP B

A village church may seem an unlikely scene of industrial development, but
the church of St Michael-in-the-Hamlet, in what is now the Liverpool
suburb of Toxteth, is of considerable interest. The architect was Thomas
Rickman, who had got together with a local ironmaster, John Cragg, and
built St George's Church at Everton in 1814 with much cast iron in the
structure. Here in 1814–15 the pair went a step further. Everything that
could be made of iron *was*, from the churchyard fence and gates to the
interior columns and arches, the window tracery and door frames, and even
the pinnacles on the tower.

Aldworth, Berkshire ☆   MAP A

The parish well-head, taking up practically all of the small village green of this remote settlement high on the chalk downs, drew water from one of the deepest wells in the country. The 372-foot shaft is now sealed, but the well-head with its elaborate winding gear remains, an awesome contraption of wood and iron housed beneath a tiled roof.

Alford, Lincolnshire ✕   MAP B

There is no law of God or nature that says that a windmill must have four sails, and the independence of millwrights is best seen in Lincolnshire, where there are several surviving mills with more than four sails. This one at Alford has five. The mill is of the type known as a tower mill, in which only the cap bearing the sails turns in the wind. The mill at Alford was built in 1837, and is still in working order. It is built of brick and has six storeys. The white-painted cap is of ogee shape and also carries the 'fantail'. This device was invented in 1746 by a miller named Lee. It is a wheel of vanes set at right angles to the sails, so that if the wind is not striking the sails, it must strike the fantail and turn the sails into the wind again. By the time this mill was built, it was possible to use an iron windshaft and gears instead of the all-timber machinery that had for centuries been such a tribute to the skills and ingenuity of millwrights and carpenters. The speed at which the grinding was done could also be controlled by changing the angle of the wooden slats in the sails.

Allenheads, Northumberland ☆   MAP B

This high moorland village is an industrial settlement developed early in the nineteenth century to house lead-miners and their families employed by the Blackett family, which had been exploiting the deposits since 1729. The abandoned workings are above a wood, west of the church of 1825 which accompanies miners' and managers' houses, school and shop, etc., which are still inhabited.

Alloa, Central ☐   MAP D

Two complete and rare glass cones survive at the glassworks here. Only five of these once plentiful buildings remain in Britain. For details of glass cones, *see* Glossary.

Alvingham, Lincolnshire ▲   MAP B

In Church Lane is an eighteenth-century corn mill now run as a working
museum. Two pairs of millstones are powered by a breastshot waterwheel
driven by the River Ludd, and can be seen grinding flour on Monday and
Thursday afternoons in August and September and some Sundays and
bank holidays. Tel: South Cockerington 544.

Amlwch, Anglesey △   MAP C

Between the A5025 and B5111 leading south from the town is Parys
Mountain, where the most spectacular remains of copper mines in Britain
can be seen. The mines had been worked since the Roman period, but
extensive exploitation began in the late eighteenth and early nineteenth
centuries, when the port of Amlwch was built to handle the copper. Fifteen
hundred men worked at one time in what became the largest copper mine
in Europe – a vast open-cast quarry hewn out of the hilltop. The local boom
in copper was over by the year of Waterloo, but mining continued until
1883, and a windmill, whose tower remains, was built to help pump water
from the quarry. Like the works at Coalbrookdale (*q.v.*) the scene here
inspired several romantic artists with its spectacle of 'sublime terror'.

Ampthill, Bedfordshire ☆   MAP A

The parish pump in the marketplace is unusual, doubling as a signpost.
The stone pillar carries an inscription to the effect that the pump was put
up by the Earl of Upper Ossory in 1785.

Anderton, Cheshire ≈   MAP B

The remarkable vertical lift here, which transports boats between the
Trent and Mersey Canal and the River Weaver about fifty feet below, is
one of the wonders of the inland waterways and a unique piece of Victorian
engineering; the only canal lift still in use in Britain. It was built in 1875 and
consists of two wrought-iron tanks or caissons in which boats are raised and
lowered by a system of counterbalance, electricity replacing the original
steam-powered hydraulic pumps. Each caisson weighed 240 tons with
water in it, and could carry one barge or two narrow boats. Nowadays
pleasure craft use the lift, going up and down within an impressive
structure of tubular iron.

Anstruther, Fife ▲

MAP D

The Scottish Fisheries Museum, at Harbourhead, has extensive exhibits on Scotland's important fishing industry, including typical fishermen's cottages and model fishing vessels. It is open daily in the summer months except Sunday mornings, and afternoons except Tuesday in winter. Tel: Anstruther 310628.

Ardeer, Strathclyde □

MAP D

On a bare peninsula between the coast and the River Garnock, west of Irvine, is the site chosen by Alfred Nobel, the Swedish discoverer of dynamite and founder of the Nobel Prizes, for an 1873 explosives factory. It is now the works of Imperial Chemical Industries, who produce most of Britain's industrial explosives, for use in quarries, mines and civil engineering works.

RICHARD ARKWRIGHT

One of the major figures of the Industrial Revolution, Arkwright was one of a poor Lancashire family of thirteen children. He was born at Preston in 1732 and got little education; he was apprenticed to a barber, and set himself up in the barbering trade at Bolton later. But with the assistance of a Warrington watchmaker, John Kay, he invented improvements to machinery used in the local cotton industry, and in 1769 patented a spinning frame, which made possible the mechanical spinning of the warp, whereas the early Spinning Jenny was only suitable for spinning the weft. Driven from his home county by the opposition of cotton workers to any machinery that seemed to threaten their livelihoods, Arkwright went to Nottingham and, in partnership with Jedediah Strutt, set up a factory to produce yarn for the knitting industry. Then in 1771 he moved to Cromford (*q.v.*) in Derbyshire, and there built a large cotton mill powered by water, which led to his spinning machine being called the 'Water Frame'. Prosperity and honour followed. Arkwright bought the manor of Cromford, was subsequently knighted, and became High Sheriff of Derbyshire – not bad for a barber's apprentice. Sir Richard Arkwright is usually regarded as the father of the factory system. He brought control and organization to a large labour force, which was ultimately to their benefit as well as his own. He died in 1792 and was buried in the church which he had built at Cromford.

Arley, Hereford & Worcester =   MAP A

The preserved and operational steam-driven Severn Valley Railway between Bewdley and Bridgnorth crosses the river at this point via a cast-iron
bridge built by Thomas Brassey in 1862. It has a flat arch of 200 foot span.

Ashover, Derbyshire □   MAP B

A squat square chimney at Stone Edge, north-west of the village, marks the
site of a lead-smelting mill established in the eighteenth century, and
entertains a dubious claim to the earliest industrial chimney in England.
The parish church, at any rate, certainly has the only lead font in
Derbyshire, despite the county's long association with lead mining.

Atcham, Shropshire +   MAP B

The bridge which formerly carried the A5 across the River Severn east of
Shrewsbury is a fine seven-arched masonry structure of 1771, and it has
been preserved alongside its modern replacement. The bridge was designed by John Gwynne, a founder-member of the Royal Academy and a
friend of Dr Johnson.

Axminster, Devon □   MAP A

The famous Axminster carpet factory, begun in 1755, still stands in Silver
Street – a stone building by the parish church, where Thomas Whitty, a
cloth weaver, began making hand-knotted wool carpets in imitation of
Turkish patterns. From his beginnings and the slightly earlier ones at
Wilton (q.v.), knowledge of carpet manufacture spread throughout the
country. The difference between a 'Wilton' and an 'Axminster' carpet,
both of which are now made by about fifty different companies in Britain, is
in the type of weave. An Axminster has its tufts inserted as a separate
operation and knotted under the warp. The firm that made carpets in the
old factory in the early nineteenth century went bankrupt, but the industry
was revived later. The modern factory, producing fine quality carpets by
machinery nowadays, can be visited on weekdays. Tel: Axminster 32244.

B Banavie, Highland ≈   MAP D

The Caledonian Canal cuts through the Great Glen to form a waterway
link between Loch Ness at Fort Augustus and Loch Linnhe near Fort

William, and in effect cuts off the North-West Highlands from the rest of
Scotland. The attractions of a sea-to-sea waterway had taxed the brains of
both James Watt (*q.v.*) and John Rennie before Thomas Telford (*q.v.*) was
commissioned by the Government in 1802 to construct the canal. Its
benefit was that shipping could avoid the dangerous passage round the
north coast of Scotland and – as Britain was at war with France – there was
great strategic value in providing a protected route for warships. The canal
took 18 years to complete, twice as long as Telford had forecast, and cost
more than double what he had estimated, but it was an outstanding
engineering achievement for the time, even though the actual length of
genuine canal that had to be dug was only 21 miles, since the navigable
channel took advantage of existing lochs along the glen. There are 29 locks
on the canal, the most interesting being here at Banavie, where the
so-called Neptune Locks form the largest 'staircase' in Britain, consisting
of 8 locks. The canal was never a commercial success, though it was made
deeper after Telford's death, but it is still open, and in the First World War
it served the strategic purpose for which it had not been needed during the
Napoleonic Wars: 70,000 mines were shipped through it, mainly by the
U.S. Navy, to protect Allied merchant shipping against German U-boats.

Bangor, Gwynedd   =   MAP C

At Penrhyn Castle, in the former stable yard, is an industrial railway
museum. The castle, in the care of the National Trust, was built with huge
profits made from slate quarrying by the first Lord Penrhyn, and the
principal exhibits in the museum are connected with transportation of the
quarry products by rail from Bethesda to Port Penrhyn.

Barmouth, Gwynedd   =   MAP C

The railway viaduct crossing the estuary of the Mawddach has a footpath
alongside, and is partly of timber construction. The bridge is nearly half a
mile long, and incorporates an iron swing bridge at the Barmouth end for
the passage of vessels on the navigable channel. A toll is payable by
pedestrians and cyclists (the bridge is not open to traffic).

Barnack, Cambridgeshire   △   MAP A

South of the village is an area known locally as 'Hills and Holes' – deserted
and overgrown quarry pits where the coarse limestone called 'ragstone' was
quarried by the Romans and widely used in medieval times. The cathedrals

of Ely and Peterborough contain much Barnack stone, and local churches and houses were built of it. The monastery at Peterborough owned the quarries in the Middle Ages, and granted quarrying rights to other abbeys for an appropriate consideration. Ramsey Abbey, for instance, paid a tribute of four thousand eels a year, during Lent, for the right to take stone from Barnack in the eleventh century. By the eighteenth century, however, the seams were exhausted and the quarries abandoned. The area is now a nature reserve.

Barnard Castle, Durham   □   MAP B

Barnard Castle was once an important centre of carpets and textiles, and at the end of Thorngate are two tall mill buildings, one of which is a weaving mill dating from 1846. Along the short tree-lined street there are several eighteenth-century three-storey weavers' cottages with the characteristic long windows to the upper-floor workshops.

Barnsley, South Yorkshire   ≈   MAP B

East of the town centre is the link between the Don Navigation and the Aire and Calder Navigation, a lock built in 1804. The Don canal was made to connect Sheffield with the Humber estuary, and various branches and inter-connections were made to the system before the coming of the railways, to make those canals serving the coal-mining and iron and steel industries some of the busiest commercial waterways in the country.

Barrow-in-Furness, Cumbria   ☆   MAP B

The ruins of the Cistercian Furness Abbey might seem, at first sight, out of place in a book of this kind, but in fact this was a medieval power-house of immense activity. Second only to Fountains in terms of wealth, Furness derived its huge income from iron-founding, sheep-farming and the export of wool. Its Chapter House was like a Board Room, where the abbots presided like chairmen of the Board, with the profit motive high on the agenda. The abbots exercised a feudal lordship over vast territories of northern England – all the Furness district, much of the Lake District and parts of Yorkshire – and they also owned land in the Isle of Man and Ireland. The monastery rebuilt the castle keep on Piel Island, whence it exported its own wool in ships built in its own dockyard there.

Bathgate, Lothian △   MAP D

West of the town is Torbane, the location where James Young discovered
the oil shale which was given the geological name Torbanite (*see* Broxburn).
A refinery was built for the industry at Pumpherston, a few miles to the east,
and opened in 1884.

Battle, East Sussex =   MAP A

The railway station at this historic town on the line between Tunbridge
Wells and Hastings is a typically extravagant piece of Victorian railway
architecture. Designed by W. Trees, it has many Gothic features, including lancet windows and a ticket office like a manorial great hall, with
beamed roof and elaborate chimneypiece.

Battle, East Sussex ☆   MAP A

The hospital, west of the town centre, was originally the Union Workhouse, or House of Industry, built in 1841 in response to the Poor Law of
1834. The gabled main block is stone-built.

Beadnell, Northumberland □   MAP B

An interesting group of lime-kilns stands beside the harbour which was
built by John Wood Craster at the end of the eighteenth century for the
export of lime. The local fishermen keep their equipment in the arched
openings nowadays.

Bedlington, Northumberland △   MAP B

In Plessey Woods along the banks of the River Blyth near Hartford Bridge
are the remains of old bell pits. These were dug as a method of extracting
coal at fairly shallow levels, and were usually only about twenty feet deep.
They were called bell pits because their shape in cross-section was like that
of a bell due to the method of working the coal. Circular shafts were dug
down to the seams and coal was then dug away from the sides until the pit
was in danger of collapsing, which it eventually did after the pit had been
abandoned.

Beeston, Cheshire ≈   MAP B

The canal lock on the Chester Canal here is unique in having its chamber
walls lined with cast-iron plates. This was Telford's answer to a problem he
was called in to solve. The lock had been built on quicksand, and gave
continual trouble as the ground subsided and water seeped away. Telford
drove piles in behind the lock walls and bolted together the iron plates to
make the lock both stable and watertight.

Beeston, Nottinghamshire ☐   MAP B

The pressures on space created in Nottingham (q.v.) by the rapid expansion of the lace industry in the nineteenth century caused the partial
dispersal of the work to other towns within easy reach of the chief centre,
and Beeston was one of the main beneficiaries. The Anglo Scotia lace
factory was built around 1870 – a Gothic four-storey building of extravagant design for such a purpose, with castellated turrets and parapet
recalling some of the fortress-like factories put up around the time of the
Luddite riots.

Beetham, Cumbria ✕   MAP B

The Heron Corn Mill on the river north of the village dates from around
1730. A breastshot waterwheel built of wood and iron, sixteen feet in
diameter, drove four pairs of millstones until the mill ceased to operate
commercially in 1955. The mill is open to the public every day except
Tuesday during the summer months. Tel: Carnforth 4903.

Belper, Derbyshire ☆   MAP B

At the junction of the A6 and A517 is North Mill, a cotton mill built in 1804
by the Strutt family, who provided work and good housing for many people
here in the eighteenth and nineteenth centuries. The mill itself was an
advanced 'fireproof' building of five storeys, constructed of brick and iron,
following the initiative of William Strutt's friend Charles Bage at Shrewsbury (q.v.). The machinery was originally powered by a large waterwheel.
The mill is still in industrial use and not open to the public.

Bembridge, Isle of Wight ✕   MAP A

The tower mill half a mile south-west of the church is the only windmill left

on the island. It is owned by the National Trust and is a permanent local
landmark. It was built of stone early in the eighteenth century and ceased to
be used in 1913. This is the simplest type of tower mill, predating more
sophisticated mills in East Anglia and elsewhere. Much of the original
wooden machinery is intact – it was used to drive two pairs of millstones for
grinding corn. The mill can be visited most days except Fridays, between
April and September. Tel: Bembridge 3945.

Berwick-upon-Tweed, Northumberland = MAP B

The Royal Border railway bridge was built by Robert Stephenson (*q.v.*) in
1847–50, 126 feet 6 inches high, with 14 arches on each of 2 tiers. It
enabled a rail link to be completed between Newcastle and Edinburgh, part
of the North-Eastern Railway promoted by George Hudson, the 'Railway
King'. The ruins of the medieval Berwick Castle were removed to make
way for the station, and some of its stone was used in the construction of the
bridge, though parts of it are of brick with stone facings.

Bestwood, Nottinghamshire △   MAP B

The name of the location was used by D.H. Lawrence in *Sons and Lovers*,
and he would have known the engine house and pithead winding gear built
in 1873 and now preserved by the county council. It stands off the A61
north of Nottingham.

Bettws-y-Coed, Gwynedd +   MAP C

Waterloo Bridge, so named because it was built in the year of the battle
(1815), is one of the oldest of the iron bridges of considerable size. It was
built by Telford (*q.v.*) to span the River Conwy at the southern edge of the
town, as part of his work on the Holyhead road, and is an extravagant
example of ironwork, cast by William Hazledine at his Plas Kynaston
foundries, where the ironwork was also cast for the aqueduct at Pont
Cysyllte (*q.v.*).

Beverley, Humberside ☆   MAP B

In the unlikely setting of Beverley Minster is an unusual piece of pre-
Industrial Revolution machinery – a treadwheel crane. It is in the roof of
the crossing tower and the south transept, and is a 1716 reconstruction of a
medieval crane. Fifteen and a half feet in diameter, it enabled a mason to
raise a quarter of a ton of stone at a time.

Bibury, Gloucestershire ▲   MAP A

Arlington Mill, in this picturesque Cotswold village astride the River Coln,
has been both a corn and fulling mill in its time. The village weavers made
cloth in the cottages of Arlington Row, converted from a fourteenth-
century monastic sheephouse, and now almshouses owned by the National
Trust. The mill itself is now a private museum devoted to cornmilling and
other rural industries, and is open to the public every day from March to
October, and at weekends in the winter months.

Bideford, Devon +   MAP A

The bridge crossing the River Torridge is nearly 680 feet long and has 24
masonry arches with spans varying between 12 and 25 feet. No two of them
are identical. This inconsistency is due to the fact that the bridge was
originally built of timber in the last quarter of the thirteenth century, and
the arches were dictated by the size of the oak beams used; then in the
fifteenth century, when the bridge was rebuilt in stone, the timber structure
was used as scaffolding and the masonry erected round it, leaving the
original wood enclosed within the stone piers and arches. This came to
light in the present century during widening and repair operations. The
money raised by the medieval trustees responsible for the upkeep of the
bridge was surplus to requirements, and enabled the bridge to become a
landowner, in which capacity it has helped the poor of the town and built
and maintained the old grammar school. A similar long bridge crosses the
Taw at Barnstaple, but this is neither as long nor as irregular as the
Bideford bridge, and has been subject to more extensive alteration.

Bingley, West Yorkshire ≈   MAP B

The Five-Rise Locks on the Leeds and Liverpool Canal, opened to traffic
in 1774, raise the level of the canal about sixty feet up the eastern side of the
Pennines. These locks are of the 'staircase' type, which are different from
'flights' of locks in that they are directly inter-connected. The bottom gate
of one lock is the top gate of the lock below it, and water passes directly
from one chamber to the next. In flights, each lock is separated from the
next by a space and has its own independent gates.

Binsted, Hampshire ☆   MAP A

Telegraph House, dating from early in the nineteenth century, was part of a chain of signal stations built to relay messages between the Admiralty in London and the Fleet at Portsmouth Dockyard during the Napoleonic Wars (*see also* Cobham). The tall white building is now a private house, having survived threats to demolish it.

Birmingham, West Midlands ☆ MAP A

In Banbury Street, east of the city centre, is the Gun Barrel Proof House. Small arms have been a speciality of Birmingham since the seventeenth century, when gunsmiths were already well established in the town, and in 1813 an Act of Parliament gave Birmingham the right to have its own proofing authority. No gun can be released for sale until its barrel has been definitively proved and stamped here. One or two nineteenth-century gunmakers' workshops survive in Birmingham's old Gun Quarter, in Bath Street and Loveday Street, and one of the local pubs is called the Gunmaker's Arms. The Proof House has an elaborate plaster insignia above its doorway, and though there is no public admittance, reliable reports tell us that barrels are still tested here.

Birmingham, West Midlands ≈ MAP A

The Gas Street Canal Basin is the terminus of the Birmingham and the Worcester and Birmingham canals, hidden near the centre of the city and the heart of a network with more miles of canal than Venice. Now a colourful scene of narrow boats with their traditional decoration, this was once a metropolis of water transport created in the late eighteenth and early nineteenth centuries to serve the rapidly expanding local industries. Victorian warehouses built round the basin have been demolished during redevelopment.

Blackburn, Lancashire □ MAP B

The Lewis Textile Museum in Exchange Street has a fine collection of cotton machinery, including working reproductions of the Spinning Jenny and Mule of Hargreaves and Crompton respectively. There are also early hand looms and power looms. Open on weekdays throughout the year. Tel: Blackburn 667130.

Blackhall Colliery, Durham ☆ MAP B

Beside the front doors of the houses at this mining settlement near

Peterlee, slates are set into the walls. Built in the days when the knocker-up came to each house to wake the workers, miners could chalk the times of their shifts on the slates so that the knocker-up could let them sleep if they were not due for work when he came by.

Blaenau Ffestiniog, Gwynedd △   MAP C

The wettest town in Britain has been a major centre of the Welsh slate industry since the eighteenth century, and the hills all round it are scarred by quarries and deformed by spoil heaps. Before open-cast working was introduced, slate was mined, and the hills were honeycombed with adits. The Industrial Revolution, which created a vast demand for urban housing, made Welsh slate an almost universal roofing material, and by the middle of the nineteenth century some 16,000 men were working in the quarries, producing roofing slates called 'duchesses' and 'countesses', among other titled ladies, according to their size. But eventually machine cutting and rival roofing materials reduced the workforce until the quarries became mere shadows of their former selves and made the area one of high unemployment. The Llechwedd Slate Caverns and the Gloddfa Ganol Slate Mine are both working quarries partly open to the public. The visitor can tour old workings and see demonstrations of the techniques involved – particularly slate cutting, in which skilled men using only a hammer and chisel can split blocks of slate into sheets one fortieth of an inch thick. Restored quarrymen's cottages at Gloddfa Ganol show the social background of the industrial workers. Both quarries are on the A470 north of the town, and are open every day during the summer months. Tel: Blaenau Ffestiniog 306 for Llechwedd and 664 for Gloddfa Ganol.

Blisworth, Northamptonshire ≈   MAP A

When the Grand Junction Canal was commenced to create a shorter route for trade in coal and other freight between the Midlands and London, the construction of a tunnel through Blisworth Hill proved to be one of the biggest engineering problems. It was begun in 1794, but the first borings were a total failure, due to unsatisfactory design and materials, and unforeseen and excessive seepage of water into the workings, and work was stopped on the proposed two-mile-long tunnel in 1796. The consultant engineer for the canal was William Jessop, and he suggested building flights of locks instead, to carry the canal over the hill, but James Barnes, the resident engineer, argued for starting a new tunnel on a different route, and in due course this was agreed. After many delays, during which the rest

Opposite
*Slate caverns
at Blaenau
Ffestiniog*

of the canal was completed and the gap closed temporarily by a horse-drawn tramway, work re-started in 1802, and the tunnel was completed in March 1805, opening the whole length of the canal to traffic. The tunnel is 3,056 yards long and is still in use.

Blyth, Northumberland   ○   MAP B

Blyth was formerly a medieval fishing and salt-working village known as Blyth Snook, which grew in the eighteenth century to become one of the north-east's great coal ports. A wagonway was constructed to carry coal from local pits to the wooden staithes – the wharves where ships lined up for loading – and brick houses were built for miners and dockers in the town that was exporting four million tons of coal a year by the end of the nineteenth century. Wooden staithes can still be seen here; among the last remaining.

Bolton, Greater Manchester   □   MAP B

Bolton was one of the first and chief centres of the cotton trade. It was here in 1770 that Samuel Crompton, a weaver, invented the 'Spinning Mule', which combined the advantages of the 'Jenny' and the 'Water Frame'. The inventions of Lancashire men for mechanizing the production of cotton goods gave rise to the familiar industrial landscape of this part of England; the tall brick-built mills which made 'King Cotton' the pride and joy of Victorian Britain. Among the typical mills of the later period is Swan Lane Mill, a seven-storey building designed and built in 1905 to accommodate nearly two hundred thousand mule spindles. It is said to have been at one time the world's largest spinning mill under one roof.

Bolton, Greater Manchester   □   MAP B

Nineteenth-century industrial settlements grew up on the north side of Bolton with the great textile boom, when wealthy mill-owners created model villages after the example of Port Sunlight (*q.v.*). One of the best here is the Barrow Bridge village, built around 1830–40 by Robert Gardner, for the workers at two mills, both of which have disappeared. But the estate itself survives, with well designed terraced houses of stone on the slopes of a wooded valley with a stream running through it. It was, said the *Illustrated London News* of the time, a 'well-organised community never equalled in the Utopias of philosophy'. Other such developments were carried out by the Ashworth brothers at Bank Top, Egerton and New Eagley, where estates were provided with schools, libraries and chapels, and each house had its own garden and piped water.

Bolton, Greater Manchester ☆   MAP B

The Tonge Moor Textile Museum in Tonge Moor Road (north-east of town centre) illustrates the history and techniques of fine cotton spinning, and exhibits include an important collection of machines, such as Crompton's 'Spinning Mule', Hargreaves' 'Spinning Jenny' and Arkwright's (q.v.) 'Water Frame'. The museum is open Monday, Tuesday and Friday all day (except bank holidays) and Saturday mornings. Tel: Bolton 21394.

Bonsall, Derbyshire □   MAP B

Bonsall was an important centre of framework knitting in Derbyshire, and one of the early workshops, where knitters worked in primitive factories instead of in their own homes, can still be seen. It is a stone building of 1737.

Boot, Cumbria ×   MAP B

Eskdale Mill, across a packhorse bridge at the north end of the village, is a corn mill driven by two overshot waterwheels, and contains an exhibition of the history and mechanics of corn milling. The mill has been restored by the county council. There is a loft where the grain used to be dried over tiles before it was ground. Open to the public from Easter to September, every day except Saturday. Tel: Kendal 21000.

Borrowdale, Cumbria △   MAP B

Above the south side of the Honister Pass between Borrowdale and Buttermere are the disused Honister slate quarries, formerly one of the chief sources of Westmorland slate, used extensively for building and roofing. Remote and isolated, the quarries were remarked on by many an unbelieving traveller in this region which Defoe called 'the wildest, most barren and frightful of any that I have passed over in England . . .' In fact, the slate from Honister was mined rather than quarried. The workers were hard-living and hard-drinking men, who left their cottage homes in the valleys on Monday mornings and did not return until Saturday nights, because their journeys to and from work were hard and hazardous, though short. The most hair-raising operation at Honister was not digging the slate, but getting it down the fells to sheds where the material was riven and dressed for transportation by packhorse to ports and river barges. The mined slate was loaded on to a wooden sledge called a 'trail-barrow'. It had two long handles called 'stangs', like the shafts of a horse-drawn wagon. A man stood between these with the barrow behind him, and came down the almost precipitous slopes with the momentum of a quarter of a ton of stone lifting him off his feet for yards at a time, the exertions of keeping the load under control leaving him breathless and throbbing. There were many accidents. The descent took only a few minutes, but then the man had to make a laborious return journey with the empty sledge, which might take half an hour. The average daily workload was seven or eight such journeys up and down. Many Lake District slate quarries are still working, but of course modern roads and vehicles make the job much less dangerous now. One place where Westmorland slate has been used to great advantage is in the new Coventry Cathedral, but it can also be seen in vernacular building, particularly at Elterwater (*q.v.*) and Troutbeck.

Boston, Lincolnshire   ○   MAP B

Several large eighteenth- and nineteenth-century granaries and warehouses survive around Boston's quays. They are mostly built of brick. Boston had been a very important port in medieval times, importing goods from the northern European ports. The large entrance lock was built in 1884 to give access to a dock which could take vessels up to three thousand tons.

Botallack, Cornwall   △   MAP A

One of the classic locations of the tin- and copper-mining industry in Cornwall, the remains of the Botallack and Levant mines are famous industrial monuments on the Land's End peninsula. The local deposits of tin and copper had been extracted from prehistoric times, the people of the Bronze Age having discovered how to make an alloy of the two metals that could be shaped into knives and tools far superior to the flint axes and other stone tools and weapons they had used hitherto. By the reign of Richard I the industry was so important to the nation that the 'Stannary' towns (from the Latin *stannum* for tin) received their own charter, awarding them their own courts and parliament and exempting them from ordinary taxes. Shaft mining began in the fifteenth century, and by the Industrial Revolution mining was being done on a large scale. Men descended to the galleries on

ladders, often made from the timbers of wrecked ships, and ore was hauled
to the surface in iron buckets called 'kibbles', and sorted from the rock by
women and children. The Botallack mine, with its nineteenth-century
engine houses spectacularly sited on the cliffs, mined tin from beneath the
sea-bed, with galleries going a third of a mile out from the shore, and the
Levant mine had men working 2,000 feet below sea level. First worked in
the 1790s, this mine had the highest production record among the local
firms. Temperatures were so high in some of the deep mines that the
'tinners' had to be sprayed with cold water while they worked in the dark
with candles fixed to their helmets. The development of steam engines
owed a lot to the tin-mining industry, because as shafts went deeper below
the surface, better means of lowering and raising men and ore and pumping
out water taxed the brains of engineers. Many Newcomen and Watt
engines were installed in Cornish mines, and Trevithick (*q.v.*) developed
engines for these purposes. Cheaply imported tin and copper from Malaya
and other parts of the world brought a decline to the Cornish trade, but it
continues on a small scale in the locality. An 1840 Cornish beam engine
remains at the Levant mine, and is preserved by the National Trust.
Application to see it must be made to the manager, as the mine is still
working. Tel: St Just 788662.

Boulby, Cleveland △   MAP B

Along the cliffs are quarries where alum was extracted from the seventeenth century until the late nineteenth century. Several remains of
treatment plants can be seen here as well as the quarries themselves. *See
also* Ravenscar. Subsequently, iron ore was also mined at Boulby, and the
foundations of a shanty town of corrugated iron huts, locally nicknamed
'Tin City', remain where miners lived until the 1930s.

Bourn, Cambridgeshire ✕   MAP A

The windmill here, restored in 1931 and open to the public, is one of the
oldest surviving in Britain. It is a black weatherboarded post mill and dates
partly from around 1635, although it was rebuilt in the eighteenth century
after gale damage. It will be noticed that the four sails are of two different
types. Two of them are 'common' sails, in which slats could be adjusted
manually according to the speed and direction of the wind. The other two
are 'patent' sails, following the invention by William Cubitt of a mechanical
device for turning the sails to regulate the speed of the driving gear.

Bournville, West Midlands ☆   MAP A

The model village commenced by Cadbury Brothers in 1893 was not intended – as was the Lever Brothers development at Port Sunlight (*q.v.*) – to be exclusively for the workers in the factory. Although it was more mundane than its northern contemporary, it had a greater influence on subsequent town planning because it was not conceived as industrial housing but as a genuine attempt to improve living conditions for the working classes and encourage independence. It was from the beginning an area of Birmingham rather than a self-contained town superimposed on the landscape, and its running and development have always been independent of the chocolate factory.

Box, Wiltshire =   MAP A

The famous Box Tunnel was one of the breathtaking engineering feats of I.K. Brunel (*q.v.*) during his construction of the Great Western Railway in the nineteenth century. It was necessary to take the line through the southern end of the Cotswold Hills to maintain the reasonably level gradient that was an essential part of his great enterprise. Brunel planned and supervised the work himself. It was an enormous tunnelling problem, and detractors called it both dangerous and impractical, because nothing on such a scale had been attempted before. The 2-mile-long tunnel took over 4 years to build, from 1836 to 1841, and at one stage 4,000 men and 300 horses were employed on it. A hundred men lost their lives. Stone excavated from the tunnel was used to build the G.W.R. locomotive workshops at Swindon (*q.v.*).

Bradford, West Yorkshire □   MAP B

The woollen industry still dominates Bradford, and among the significant buildings of the city's nineteenth-century industry are Manningham Mills and the so-called 'Little Germany' warehouses. The palatial Manningham Mills were built by Samuel Lister in 1873. Lister was the inventor of several mechanical processes which made his fortune, and he duly became Lord Masham. The Lister Comb, patented in 1851, was the first machine to comb long fibred wools. In these six-storey mills velvet and plush were made. The mills are in Heaton Road, and the boilerhouse chimney, 255 feet high, is in the style of a Venetian campanile and is known locally as Lister's Pride. The warehouses known as the 'Little Germany' are so called because of their flamboyant architectural style. They are in Vicar Lane,

Well Street and Peckover Street, and were built from 1853 onwards to supplement the old Piece Hall (now demolished), which could no longer contain all the wool traders.

Bradford, West Yorkshire ☆ MAP B

Bradford's Industrial Museum, in Moorside Road, occupies a multi-storey former worsted spinning mill, and appropriately enough is concerned chiefly with the local textile industry, demonstrating the conversion of raw wool into worsted material and showing the general history of the wool trade. There is also a waterwheel in working order, and a stationary steam engine, as well as examples of local public transport which include the only remaining Bradford tram. Open every day except Mondays and winter bank holidays. Tel: Bradford 631756.

Bradford, West Yorkshire □ MAP B

The Yorkshire wool trade gave rise to a good deal of flamboyant building, which says something about the nature of Yorkshiremen as well as about the immense wealth of the industry. The neo-Gothic Wool Exchange (still used for trading in wool by dealers from home and abroad) in Market Street is a Victorian extravaganza built in 1864–7 by the architects Lockwood and Mawson, who also designed Bradford's Town Hall.

Bradford-on-Tone, Somerset ▲ MAP A

At Three Bridges Farm, on the A38 south-east of the village, R.J. Sheppy & Son are independent cider-makers in the traditional home of cider, the flat lands of Somerset where thousands of acres of orchards produce apples with unfamiliar names to the greengrocer and the supermarket, like Slack-ma-Girdle and Bloody Butcher. The popularity of cider seems to have grown up around the time of the Norman Conquest, and the best soil and climate for growing apples dictated that the south-west became predominant in cider-making. Until mass production, the art of cider-making was a sideline of farmers' wives. The apples were harvested in autumn by using long poles to shake the branches of the trees, and then reduced to pulp in a cider mill, which might vary from a small hand machine to a large mill driven by horsepower. Then the pulp was crushed to extract the juice, and the liquid was left for up to three months to ferment before being transferred to casks for maturing. The principles remain the same today, but the processes have been made more speedy and economic-

al by mechanized methods, including the harvesting of the apples. Here
you can see the works and a museum and buy the product. The farm is open
daily from April to December. Tel: Bradford-on-Tone 233.

Bressingham, Norfolk ☆   MAP A

The Bressingham Steam Museum is a splendid private collection of
railway locomotives, traction engines and stationary steam engines, open to
the public on Sunday, Thursday and bank holiday afternoons in the
summer months. Tel: Bressingham 386.

Bridgnorth, Shropshire =   MAP B

The town is built on two levels, above and below a ridge of sandstone which
rises from the west bank of the River Severn, and a remarkable cliff railway,
called Castle Hill Railway, was built in 1892 to link High Town with Low
Town. It is the only inland funicular railway in this country, and is still in
operation, its cars travelling up and down a gradient of 1–1½ and worked
nowadays by electric motor. When first built they were driven by a
water-balance system.

Brierley Hill, West Midlands ≈   MAP A

The Black Delph Locks are an impressive flight of eight close but separate
locks, rebuilt in 1858 to link the Stourbridge Canal with the Dudley Canal
– part of the intricate transport system for industry in the Midlands,
developed in the late eighteenth century, which linked the Severn with
Birmingham and London, and carried glass from Stourbridge (*q.v.*) as well
as coal and other goods.

Brill, Buckinghamshire ×   MAP A

The photogenic windmill standing on a knoll at the north-west side of the
village is a post mill dating from around 1680, and is among the oldest in
England. A weatherboarded flour mill, it was originally supported on open
timberwork, but this has been enclosed within a brick roundhouse. The
mill's machinery is intact, and can be seen on Sunday afternoons in
summer. The uneven ground around the mill was created by digging clay
for brick-making.

JAMES BRINDLEY

Called the 'father of English canals', Brindley was originally a millwright by trade, born in Derbyshire in 1716 and barely educated, but showing a natural genius for engineering in an age when that word was scarcely part of the vocabulary. He was asked to survey the possibilities of a canal to connect the Mersey with the Trent, and he began to conceive an inland waterway system that would link the rivers Thames, Severn, Trent and Mersey. Meanwhile he was commissioned by the Duke of Bridgewater to build a canal linking the duke's coal mines at Worsley (*q.v.*) with Manchester. The characteristic feature of Brindley's canals was their winding routes, following contours as far as possible without involving major earthworks. This was not merely to avoid high costs on difficult engineering problems, but to link as many villages as convenient with a system of transport, something that could only be done previously with wagons or packhorses. Many of Brindley's ideas were regarded as the hair-brained schemes of a madman which would never see the light of day. Brindley died in Staffordshire in 1772, and although he did not live to see the realization of his dream, his was the unlettered genius that set the great age of canal-building in motion.

Bristol, Avon ○   MAP A

In Great Western Dock, Gas Ferry Road, is the *SS Great Britain*, the first screw-driven ocean-going liner built of iron. This dry dock was built specially for the construction of the ship by Brunel (*q.v.*). She was launched in 1843 by Prince Albert, and was the largest ship then afloat. The hull was made of overlapping wrought-iron plates riveted to metal frames. The ship could carry over 1,000 tons of coal to fuel her transatlantic voyages, and accommodated more than 250 passengers. She served her masters well until 1886, when she was abandoned as a hulk in the Falkland Islands. Almost a century later, she was salvaged and brought back to Bristol with money raised by the Great Britain Steamship Preservation Project, and now occupies her original dock in restored state and welcomes visitors aboard. The ship is open daily.

Bristol, Avon ○   MAP A

Space does not permit a listing of all the fascinating maritime relics of Bristol's historic dockland. Modern commercial shipping docks downriver from the city at Portishead and Avonmouth, but much of interest remains preserved at the City Docks. Bristol's position at the mouths of the Avon and Severn, facing the Atlantic Ocean, gave it importance as a port many centuries ago, and Bristol mariners were in the forefront of maritime commerce. John and Sebastian Cabot and Martin Frobisher set sail on their pioneering voyages from here. The modern dock system at Bristol was largely the work of William Jessop early in the nineteenth century, with later alteration and expansion by Brunel (*q.v.*). After the decline of the port, largely as a result of the abolition of slavery, this modernization once again allowed Bristol to compete with other great commercial docks such as Liverpool and London (*qq.v.*). A wrought-iron girder swing bridge at the Northern Entrance Lock may be the original installed by Brunel. At Wapping Wharf is a steam crane with a curved jib, built in 1875 and now preserved as an industrial exhibit – the only one of its kind left. Several warehouses and other buildings display the architectural style peculiar to the district in the nineteenth century. It became known as 'Bristol Byzantine' because of the ogee arches commonly used over windows.

Bristol, Avon ☆ MAP A

Outside the Corn Exchange are four flat-topped pillars like garden bird-tables with brass tops. They have stood here since the seventeenth century, and were originally in front of the Council House which was known as the Tolzey. The pillars are actually called Nails, and on them merchants used to complete their financial deals before the Exchange was built. From this practice comes the phrase 'paying on the nail'.

Bristol, Avon ☆ MAP A

Beneath Denmark Street, west of the city centre, are extensive cellars, dating back to the thirteenth century and once part of an Augustinian monastery. They now belong to Harveys of Bristol, and are used as a wine museum, displaying tools and casks and the history of wine and sherry. The cellars are open to the public on Fridays only. Tel: Bristol 277661.

Bromsgrove, Hereford & Worcester = MAP A

In the churchyard are the graves of two young railwaymen killed in 1840 by a boiler explosion at Bromsgrove Station on the Birmingham and Gloucester Railway. Contemporary locomotives are carved on their headstones, which also bear nauseating rhyming epitaphs of the kind so beloved by the Victorians.

Broughton-in-Furness, Cumbria □   MAP B

In the woods near Duddon Bridge, a mile west of the town, are the remains of a charcoal blast furnace, with some ruined buildings and workers' dwellings nearby. These ironworks were built in 1736 and were worked for 130 years, exploiting local iron ore deposits. The furnace was charged from above, and the bellows operated by the water of the River Duddon, directed through a leat. Coppices of oak were cultivated in the area for the provision of charcoal.

Broxburn, Lothian △   MAP D

North of the village are the 'bings' or spoil-heaps of an important but relatively short-lived Scottish chemical industry – the extraction of oil from shale. Dr James Young, an associate of Michael Faraday, first mined the shale in 1851 at Torbane and refined paraffin from it, and the discovery started a sort of gold rush to the Lothians, where many small firms rose and soon fell. Oil shale was also called 'boghead coal', and for a time Scotland supplied ninety per cent of the world's shale oil output.

ISAMBARD KINGDOM BRUNEL

The word 'genius' may be overworked, but if anyone mentioned in this book was entitled to it, it surely must be Brunel. He was born at Portsmouth in 1806, the only son of the civil engineer and inventor Sir Marc Isambard Brunel, who was born in France and left his native country at the Revolution. Isambard himself went to Paris to study at the age of fourteen, and after three years returned to join his father's firm. By the time he was twenty he was working with his father on the construction of the Thames Tunnel; in 1831 he was put in charge of the suspension bridge at Clifton (*q.v.*) which he had designed; and in 1833 he became chief engineer of the Great Western Railway, which was largely his brainchild. He did not merely jump on the bandwagon of the great railway boom, but rethought the whole business from scratch and – with sound reasoning – adopted a broad gauge (7 feet) which only had to be converted to the 'standard' gauge of 4 feet 8½ inches after nearly sixty years because it had become isolated from the rest of the country's railway network. Brunel was a successful naval architect, and an outstanding builder of bridges and tunnels, to say nothing of his three great steamships, the *Great Western*, which sailed out of the Bristol Channel to open up the first regular passenger service between Europe and America; the *Great Britain* (*see* Bristol); and the *Great Eastern*, which began its maiden voyage a few days before Brunel's death in 1859, and remained the largest ship afloat for nearly half a century. The graves of both Brunels are in London's Kensal Green Cemetery. There is a statue of I.K. Brunel in the new town centre at Swindon (*q.v.*) and another on London's Victoria Embankment, but his real monuments are the great engineering works still in use which are scattered through this book.

Bucklers Hard, Hampshire   ○   MAP A

On the west bank of the Beaulieu River lies this famous and attractive village which once had an important dockyard, building naval warships of New Forest oak. The second Duke of Montagu had planned to make Bucklers Hard into a port rivalling Southampton. His scheme failed, of course, but for a century, from 1749 when Henry Adams started building ships here, it was a flourishing dockyard. There is little to be seen of the former docks now, only depressions marked with stakes identifying the site, but the village remains, where some of the master shipwrights lived who built Nelson's favourite ship, *HMS Agamemnon*, as well as many other men o' war for the British fleet. The wide eighteenth-century street running down to the riverside has grass verges in front of two long terraces of brick cottages. Stacks of weathering timber stood between them in the days when four thousand men worked in the shipyard at the height of the Napoleonic Wars. There is a Maritime Museum here now, and the former house of the Master Shipbuilder, Henry Adams, is an hotel.

Bucksburn, Grampian   □   MAP D

Stoneywood Mill, by the River Don, is an important paper-making mill in Scotland, where a large proportion of Britain's paper is made. The industry grew up on the strength of local timber and water supplies. Logs of coniferous trees are ground down to produce a cellulose fibre for what is called mechanical wood pulp, used to make cheap paper such as newsprint. Finer papers are made by chemical processing which removes impurities from the pulp. Stoneywood Mill dates back to the eighteenth century, and is now part of the Wiggins Teape Group. It can produce up to forty thousand tons of paper a year. Visitors can tour the mill by prior arrangement. Tel: Aberdeen 712841.

Burnley, Lancashire   □   MAP B

At Harle Syke, just outside the town to the north-east, Queen Street Mill, which used to be a cotton mill, has been preserved by the local council in association with Pennine Heritage, and the building's steam engine, which powered the looms, remains *in situ* and in working order. It can be seen at certain times. Tel: Burnley 59996.

Burslem, Staffordshire □   MAP B (*Stoke-on-Trent*)

The Wedgwood Memorial Institute in Queen Street was built 1863–9 and is a typical Victorian extravaganza of brick and terracotta. Mr Gladstone laid the foundation stone. It stands on the site of Wedgwood's first factory, and has a statue of him over the porch, as well as a series of elaborate reliefs and friezes. Members of the Wedgwood family had been master potters here since the seventeenth century, and Burslem has been called the 'Mother of the Potteries'. Among the many firms still working here is Price's Teapot Works. Nearby is the Trent and Mersey Canal, of which Josiah Wedgwood (*q.v.*) was one of the promoters, realizing the value of a better transport system between his factories and the docks at Liverpool. Pottery materials continued to be carried on the canal until the 1960s. One or two bottle ovens survive in the district (*see* Glossary).

Burton-on-Trent, Staffordshire ▲   MAP B

Burton-on-Trent is one of the chief centres of the brewing industry, and legend has it that the origin of its pre-eminence was the discovery by a medieval monk that water pumped from the local sandstone after seeping through deposits of gypsum gave beer an excellent flavour. Among the first to exploit this property on an industrial scale in the eighteenth century were William Worthington and William Bass, and when trade marks began to be registered under the Trade Marks Act of 1875, the very first was William Bass's familiar red triangle. A three-storey nineteenth-century building of the Bass company, off Horninglow Street, is now a museum of the brewing industry. The history and method of brewing is shown, and exhibits include a model brewery and the Bass company's own steam locomotive. Elsewhere in the town, several maltings with their kilns can be seen. Once barley has been converted to malt, brewing consists of boiling the liquid produced by steeping malt in hot water with the hops that give the beer its bitter taste. Then it is put in large vessels where yeast is added to convert sugar to alcohol. Finally it is stored in casks for a time which varies according to the final requirements, since pale and bitter ales take longer to mature than mild ales. The Bass museum is open throughout the year, and is situated north of the town centre. Tel: Burton 42031.

C Caldbeck, Cumbria □   MAP B

In the Howk, an eerie limestone gorge reached by a pleasant few minutes'
walk from the southern corner of the village green, is the threadbare ruin of
a bobbin mill. Bobbin-making was originally a coppice industry – one of
those that depended on a small plantation of selected trees for commercial
use – in this case birch. Bobbin-making throve on the rise of the cotton
industry in Lancashire, and it was the invention of John Braithwaite of a
bobbin-making machine that turned the craft into a factory industry. The
greatest concentration of bobbin mills was in the Furness district of what
was then north Lancashire, and in the mid-nineteenth century more than
fifty mills were at work in the region, making half the bobbins used in the
entire textile industry of Britain. The mills needed fast-flowing rivers to
run their machinery – hence the presence of a mill in such a secluded and
unlikely industrial site.

Calstock, Cornwall   =   MAP A

On the Cornish side of the Tamar, the village is dominated by the railway
viaduct crossing the river. It was built in 1907 to serve the local soft fruit
trade, and although it is an elegant bridge it is actually built of concrete
blocks which were made on the site. The viaduct is over 1,000 feet long and
the crossing stands more than 100 feet above the river, with 12 arches of
60-foot span.

Calver, Derbyshire   □   MAP B

Between the village and Curbar, to the east, is Calver Mill. It was one of the
earliest cotton mills, built in 1785. It was constructed of stone on six storeys
and had circular cast-iron pillars, the characteristic square-headed windows with small panes of glass, staircase turrets like those in medieval
castles and manor houses, and a wheel house from which a waterwheel
drove the machinery. Some rebuilding was carried out in 1804, after the
earlier building had been damaged by fire (*see* Shrewsbury), for it had
timber floors, but the main block is basically the same as originally built,
and is still in use.

Calverton, Nottinghamshire   □   MAP B

A curate of Calverton in the late sixteenth century, Rev. William Lee, had a
brainwave one day when sitting at home watching his wife knitting

stockings by hand. He invented a machine which made the job quicker and easier by providing a separate needle for each loop, so as to make a whole row of stitches at one operation instead of casting all the loops on to one needle. Invented in 1589, when Elizabeth I was on the throne of England, the 'stocking frame' came into use when the demand for stockings was from both sexes, and it signalled the birth of a great industry, although recognition of its revolutionary potential was slow in coming, and William Lee died penniless in Paris. The opposition of knitters to increasing mechanization was to be a continuing theme in the hosiery industry for more than two centuries, culminating in the so-called Luddite Rebellion. Until the rise of factory industry, framework knitting was a cottage industry, and in Calverton (in Windles Square and elsewhere), Ruddington (*q.v.*) and many other Midland towns and villages, knitters' cottages can still be seen. The characteristic cottage was brick-built on two storeys with a long window on the upper floor where the wooden frame stood to give the operator maximum light.

Camborne, Cornwall ☆ MAP A

At Penponds, half a mile south-west of the town centre, is the cottage in which Richard Trevithick (*q.v.*) was born in 1771. It is owned by the National Trust (identified by their sign) and occupied by a tenant who will show the cottage to interested visitors on application at reasonable times.

Cambridge, Cambridgeshire + MAP A

The Magdalene Bridge over the River Cam is a cast-iron structure of 1823. It replaced an eighteenth-century bridge of stone.

Cardiff, South Glamorgan ☆ MAP C

The National Museum of Wales, close to the city centre, has an important industrial section with exhibits on the coal, iron and steel industries, in particular, illustrating both the history of the industries and some of their techniques. In Bute Street, the Welsh Industrial and Maritime Museum exhibits some large machinery, including steam engines, used in various industries and public services. Both museums are open throughout the year except Sunday mornings and some bank holidays. Tel: National Museum, Cardiff 397951; Industrial Museum, Cardiff 481919.

Carew, Dyfed ✕   MAP C

A corn mill on the River Cleddau here is interesting as a rare surviving example of a tide mill. It dates from the eighteenth century and is built on three storeys, and, though no longer in commercial use, it is maintained as a working museum. River water is 'captured' at high tide by a barrage, and the controlled ebb then turns the waterwheel to drive the machinery.

Carisbrooke, Isle of Wight ☆   MAP A

In the bailey of Carisbrooke Castle is a well house containing a donkey wheel, built in 1587 to draw water from the well which was sunk probably in 1270, to a depth of about 160 feet. The diameter of this, one of a few surviving treadwheels, is 15½ feet. It is not as large as the wheel at Rotherfield Greys (q.v.) but is sometimes put in operation with a donkey, as a tourist attraction. The castle is in the care of the Department of the Environment, and is open to visitors throughout the year, except Sunday mornings and some bank holidays.

Carnforth, Lancashire =   MAP B

The 'Steamtown' railway museum in Warton Road has a collection of railway paraphernalia and some British and European steam locomotives, including the 'Flying Scotsman'. Carnforth grew up as a railway town from 1857. The museum is open daily. Tel: Carnforth 4220.

Carthew, Cornwall △   MAP A

At this village north of St Austell is the Wheal Martyn China Clay Works, now preserved as an open-air museum of the industry that brought prosperity to this part of Cornwall from the mid-eighteenth century, when William Cookworthy, a Plymouth Quaker and apothecary, discovered kaolin, the chief ingredient of porcelain, which had been a secret closely guarded by the Chinese for over a thousand years. Kaolin, or 'china clay', is formed by the decomposition of granite, and Cornwall and Dartmoor were found to have huge deposits which were soon exploited on a large scale. The eerie lunar landscape of white spoil-heaps around St Austell is explained by the fact that there are eight tons of waste to every ton of china clay extracted. It seems odd, at first sight, that the potteries of Stoke-on-Trent (q.v.) should have grown up more than two hundred miles away from the source of their vital ingredient, but in fact the manufacture of stoneware

Opposite
*Thrang Quarry
at Chapel Stile* and earthenware had been established in Staffordshire long before the secret of porcelain was found, and that area had the necessary clay, coal and water supplies for the growth of the industry. Nowadays, in any case, only a small proportion of the china clay extracted in Cornwall is used in pottery. By far the largest quantities are used in paper-making, and kaolin is also used in the manufacture of paint, cosmetics and drugs, among other things. The Wheal Martyn works ceased commercial production in 1968, but visitors can now see the whole history and process of producing china clay, as well as the machinery used, which included a huge breastshot water-wheel of 35 feet diameter, to drive pumps in the quarry pit. The museum is open from April to October. Tel: Stenalees 850362.

Catcliffe, South Yorkshire □   MAP B

Europe's oldest remaining glass cone, dating from the mid-eighteenth century, stands here where William Fenney started his own glass works in 1740 after experience as a works manager on the other side of Sheffield. The brick and stone-built cone is sixty feet high, and was saved from demolition in 1962 by excavations which showed its importance as an industrial monument, this area of Yorkshire once having had a thriving glass industry. For the technique of making glass in cones, *see* Stourbridge.

Chapel Allerton, Somerset ✕   MAP A

At this village near Wedmore, less well known, perhaps, than its Yorkshire namesake, is one of the few complete surviving windmills in the West Country. Known as Ashton Mill, it is an impressive white tower mill of conical shape, built of the local limestone and having a wooden cap bearing the sails which could be turned into the wind by a hand-operated chain drive. The former corn mill is owned by Bristol City Museum and is open to the public.

Chapel Stile, Cumbria △   MAP B

This village and its neighbour Elterwater (*q.v.*) are old quarrying villages, and from the church at Chapel Stile you can walk up a footpath which leads to the dramatic Thrang Slate Quarry. It seems to hang threateningly over the village, with massive detached boulders of slate ready to topple if you put a foot wrong, and great heaps of rubble lie where they were detached from the rock face by gunpowder, which was also made in the vicinity.

Charlestown, Cornwall ○

This little harbour near St Austell is named after Charles Rashleigh, who built it in the late eighteenth century to a design by John Smeaton. There were only 9 inhabitants of the hamlet called Porthmeor before the harbour was created, but within 10 years the population had risen to nearly 300. The harbour's purpose was to ship china clay and copper from Rashleigh's quarries and mines, and it was enlarged twice during its early years of operation. Later on, Welsh coal began to be imported here as well. China clay is still exported from the quay.

Chatham, Kent ○

Various naval buildings at Chatham Dockyard, established in 1546 by Henry VIII, date from the late eighteenth or early nineteenth century. The Royal Navy no longer uses Chatham, but among other buildings, its sawmills and hemp store remain, dating from around 1812. The sawmills were built and fitted out by Sir Marc Brunel, father of Isambard Kingdom Brunel (*q.v.*). The Ropery (not surprisingly, where ropes were made) is a three-storey building of 1785, over a thousand feet long without any internal partitions.

Cheddleton, Staffordshire □

The Cheddleton Flint Mill was established in the eighteenth century to supply the Potteries (*see* Stoke-on-Trent) with one of their raw materials, crushed flint. The complex has been restored by a voluntary trust, and comprises two grinding mills with a wharf and crane on the Caldon Canal; flint was delivered to the works by barge on the canal after coming all the way from south-east England where it mostly occurs. The mill's machinery was powered by waterwheels, one of which – a breastshot wheel of 22 feet diameter – has been fully restored. Crushed flint was used mainly in the manufacture of superior earthenware, which was being made in the Potteries before china and porcelain. Open weekend afternoons throughout the year.

Cheltenham, Gloucestershire △

South of the town at Leckhampton is the so-called Devil's Chimney, a grotesquely shaped pillar of rock which is a prominent local landmark. The rock is actually quarrying residue in one of the oldest and most productive areas of Cotswold quarrying of the Jurassic limestone belt which has produced building stone since the reign of Edward III. Much of central Cheltenham was built out of this deep bed of fine-grained Oolitic limestone.

Chester, Cheshire ☐ MAP B

Those readers who remember the 1951 Festival of Britain in London will no doubt recall the shot tower which attracted much attention at the time. It was built in 1826 and stood near Waterloo Bridge. It was demolished soon afterwards in the redevelopment of what is now known as the South Bank. The only remaining shot tower in the country now is at Chester, among the buildings of Associated Lead at Boughton, east of the city centre. Shot towers were devised in the eighteenth century for the casting of lead shot. Molten lead was mixed with arsenic and poured through a sort of outsize colander from a great height into a tank of water. The drops of liquid solidified during the fall and were instantly cooled by the water, which also preserved the shot from damage by impact on a hard surface.

Chipping Norton, Oxfordshire ☐ MAP A

At the western outskirts of the town is the Bliss Valley Tweed Mill, an imposing stone-built factory which, if it were not for its chimney rising from a domed tower, would look like a great country mansion. The mill was built in 1872 to the design of an architect, George Woodhouse, who specialized in textile mills and came, not surprisingly perhaps, from Bolton, Lancashire. The obligatory factory clock is on the tower below the dome.

Chirk, Shropshire ≈ MAP B

Although not so spectacular as his famous aqueduct at Pont Cysyllte (*q.v.*), Chirk Aqueduct, built in 1796–1801 to carry the Ellesmere Canal across the River Ceirog, is still one of the fine pieces of engineering work carried out by Thomas Telford (*q.v.*). It has ten arches each of forty foot span, and the masonry structure supports a cast-iron trough carrying the canal.

Clayton, West Sussex = MAP A

At the northern end of the Clayton tunnel, built in 1840 to carry the London–Brighton line under the South Downs, is a castellated portal of yellow brick, characteristic of the flamboyant design of the Victorian railway mania. But the most extraordinary aspect of this portal is that there is a cottage sitting right on top of it, flanked by neo-Gothic turrets. (Above the hill are two windmills, known as Jack and Jill, although built fifty years apart, one pre-dating and one post-dating the tunnel.)

Clifton, Avon   +   MAP A

In this district of Bristol, two miles west of the city centre, is the famous suspension bridge crossing the Avon Gorge 245 feet above the river. A competition was held for the design of the proposed toll bridge in 1829, and from 22 entries the winner was a young engineer named I.K. Brunel (*q.v.*). He was then in his early twenties. One of the judges was Thomas Telford (*q.v.*), by then in his seventies. Work began on the bridge in 1836, with Brunel himself in charge, but money ran out after four years and the project was abandoned. After Brunel's death, and in more prosperous times, work was recommenced on a modified design, as a tribute to the great man whose career as an independent engineer had begun with this project, and the bridge was finally opened to traffic in 1864. This most elegant of bridges has a centre span of 702 feet.

Clydebank, Strathclyde   ○   MAP D

Little more than a century ago, most of the river bank where huge shipyards now stand was fertile agricultural land. It was the availability of local steel and the advent of steam power that gave Glasgow the incentive to dredge and widen the river in order to transform its few old boatyards into one of the world's great shipbuilding centres. From the middle of the nineteenth century, Glasgow's population rocketed, to make it Britain's third largest city, and its docks and shipyards stretched westward from the Govan and Clydebank districts towards the estuary as far as Port Glasgow and Greenock (*q.v.*). The first ocean-going ship with a steam engine – Henry Bell's *Comet* – was launched from Port Glasgow in 1812, and the best known of the Clyde's ships were always the ocean liners, though the yards built merchant ships, warships for the Royal Navy and many other types of vessel. John Brown's shipyard at Clydebank became famous with the launching of Cunard's liner *Lusitania*, followed by *Queen Mary*, *Queen Elizabeth* and, ultimately, *QE2*. Clydebank's industrial landscape can be seen from the A814 passing the north bank of the river from Glasgow to the west.

Coalbrookdale, Shropshire ☆   MAP B

Coalbrookdale, now absorbed by the New Town of Telford, was formerly an industrial village in the heavily wooded Severn valley subsequently called the Ironbridge Gorge (*q.v.*). Some of the earliest charcoal blast furnaces in England were built in this vicinity, where iron ore was mined on the edge of the Shropshire coalfield, and the trees provided charcoal for smelting. But the demand for timber was so great, for use in building houses, machinery, furniture and so on, that it outstripped the supply, and ironmasters were aware of the need to find new techniques for the mass-production of iron. Instead of smelting the ore with charcoal in slow processes aided by waterwheels, they needed to do it with cheap coke produced by the rapidly expanding coal-mining industry. It was the Quaker ironmaster Abraham Darby (*q.v.*) who first used this method successfully here in 1709, and in so doing, he made Coalbrookdale the cradle of the Industrial Revolution and Shropshire – for a time – the centre of the industrial world, with ideal coal deposits at hand to give the area a head start in the production of pig-iron. The Coalbrookdale iron works were soon involved with Newcomen's (*q.v.*) and Watt's steam engines, with Trevithick's locomotive, and with Brunel's steam ships. Artists such as Turner, Cotman and John Martin came here to record the fiery scenes of the 'satanic mills' whose blast-furnaces belched flames into the sky and seemed to the Romantics something like visions of hell. But within a century, the Coalbrookdale iron industry had collapsed. Mineral resources were being run down, communications and transport were inadequate to keep the area in the forefront of the industry, and soon furnaces were being blown out and forges closed down. The area where the Industrial Revolution had received its greatest impetus was soon one of high unemployment. Soup kitchens were more numerous than blast furnaces, and Coalbrookdale declined almost into an industrial ghost town. Some of the most significant work of industrial archaeology has been done here since 1959, and the industrial buildings and relics of the district are in the hands of the Ironbridge Gorge Museum (*q.v.*). A walk round the streets of Coalbrookdale and its former satellites – Ironbridge (*q.v.*), Broseley, Madeley, Jackfield, etc. – is a fascinating experience of lost industrial greatness, with long terraces of brick-built houses, Nonconformist chapels, and cast-iron gravestones in the churchyards.

Coalport, Shropshire ☐   MAP B

John Rose set up the famous porcelain factory at Coalport in 1785, and it

Opposite
*Coalport China
Works Museum*
became noted for the fine quality of its decoration and lavish gilding. In 1820 the firm won a Gold Medal from the Royal Society of Arts for its introduction of a feldspathic glaze to replace the lead glaze which had caused one of the occupational hazards of workers in the china industry, the disease they called 'potter's rot'. Five hundred people were employed by the company in the mid-nineteenth century, but after various changes in ownership, the Coalport business was moved to Staffordshire after the First World War, though the name was retained and the firm continued to prosper. It now belongs to the Wedgwood group. Some of the buildings here were demolished, but what remained has been restored and is now a working museum of the industry within the Ironbridge Gorge Museum (*q.v.*). The old bottle kilns have been preserved, and visitors can see the techniques of china manufacture as well as a display of fine Coalport china. Open daily throughout the year. Tel: Ironbridge 3522.

Coates, Gloucestershire ≈   MAP A

Half a mile south-west of the village, near the railway line, is the eastern portal of the Sapperton Tunnel, 2¼ miles long. The tunnel was built in the 1780s to carry the Thames and Severn Canal through the high ground of Hailey Wood. The portal is of local limestone and classical design, with attached Doric columns flanking the round arch. The canal's purpose was to link the Stroudwater Navigation with the Thames and thus provide an inland waterway from the Black Country to London via the Severn, but it was never a commercial success and was finally abandoned in the early years of the present century. Restoration of some sections is taking place, however. Several men were killed during construction of the tunnel. In Hailey Wood large mounds of earth with beech growing on them are spoil-heaps where shafts were driven in the course of building to provide air vents.

Cobham, Surrey ☆   MAP A

At Chatley Heath, south-west of the village, is a brick tower built in 1823 to relay messages passed by semaphore between Portsmouth and the Admiralty in London. Telegraph Tower is hardly impressive architecture, though five storeys high and of hexagonal shape. It replaced an earlier telegraph station built of timber on the site, and remained in use until 1847 when it was superseded by the electric telegraph and later the telephone. The tower is privately owned and not open to the public. Another telegraph station in the chain is at Pewley Hill, Guildford, and is now a private dwelling called Semaphore House.

Colchester, Essex ✕   MAP A

In Bourne Road, a mile south of the town centre, is Bourne Mill, now a property of the National Trust. It was originally built in 1591 as a fishing lodge, and was purchased by Dutch immigrants in the seventeenth century for use as a cloth mill. The single-storey brick and stone building has eccentric stepped gables with convex and concave curves and little pinnacles. The nineteenth century saw the mill converted to flour milling, with three pairs of millstones driven by an overshot waterwheel of 22 foot diameter, and it was probably then that a weatherboarded hoist loft was added to the building. The machinery is in working order, and can be seen on Wednesday and weekend afternoons in summer, or by written appointment with the tenant.

Colchester, Essex ☆   MAP A

One of Colchester's most prominent buildings is a top-heavy Victorian water tower, known locally as Jumbo, standing beyond the western end of High Street. This architectural monstrosity was built of red brick in 1882, and is over a hundred feet high.

Coldstream, Borders +   MAP D

The five-arched masonry bridge across the Tweed linking England and Scotland at Coldstream was built in 1763 by John Smeaton, builder of one of the Eddystone lighthouses (see Plymouth). He adopted the same principle in the spandrels as William Edwards had used eight years before at Pontypridd (q.v.), lightening the load with hollow tunnels through the rubble infilling.

Congleton, Cheshire ≈   MAP B

The Macclesfield Canal, which was built to serve the growing textile and other industries of Macclesfield and Congleton, was one of the final attempts to hold at bay the growing threat to canal transport from the railways. The original plans were made by Telford (q.v.) though he had little to do with the canal's construction. At Congleton the canal is carried over a road at the south-east side of the town by a cast-iron aqueduct, built around 1835, on curving masonry abutments.

Coniston, Cumbria △   MAP B

The fells above Coniston have long been a source of the widely used
Westmorland slate (*see* Borrowdale), but the mountain known as Coniston
Old Man and its associated fells are equally interesting as an area of
copper-mining activity, and one nearby location is known as Coppermines
Valley. Large-scale mining of copper began in Britain under Queen
Elizabeth I, with the establishment of the Society of Mines Royal which had
a monopoly in copper trading and was responsible for bringing many
German miners to this country. The German engineer Höchstetter was
one of the first experts to exploit the local deposits on an industrial scale.
The mined ore had to be transported by packhorse to Keswick for smelting.
Copper mining was a highly profitable business, but it did not please
everyone. The operations caused flooding and pollution, and the modern
problem of industrial waste disposal was a heated topic here in the
seventeenth century. Most of the mining remains to be found date from the
nineteenth century, during the last period of activity before cheaper foreign
copper brought about the decline and fall of the local industry. The railway
was brought to Coniston in 1859 mainly to transport copper and slate. The
best site is about a mile and a half north-west of Coniston village in the
upper valley of Church Beck, where there is a Youth Hostel, but many
other disused sites are scattered about. There are dangerous shafts,
however, and great caution must be exercised in exploring the mining
remains.

Cononley, North Yorkshire △   MAP B

The tall engine house of a former lead mine remains west of the village. It
was built in 1832 to pump water from the workings.

Consett, Durham △   MAP B

South of the modern steel town off the A692 a deep ravine called Hownes
Gill has some 'caves', which were actually the entrances to stone mines.
The sandstone was quarried here at first, but later mined when this was
found to be more economical than removing the 'overburden' – the rock
and soil which has to be dug away in quarrying to get at the useful strata.

Conwy, Gwynedd +   MAP C

The suspension bridge across the estuary of the River Conwy was built by

Telford (*q.v.*) and opened to traffic in 1826. It has a span of 327 feet between suspension towers of stone which Telford designed like medieval battlemented gateways, as the bridge is so close to the ancient Conwy Castle. The bridge is now used only by pedestrians, having been superseded by a new road bridge in 1958. Also alongside it is a tubular railway bridge, built in 1848 by Robert Stephenson (*q.v.*).

Corby, Northamptonshire □   MAP A

A hundred years ago, Corby was a little country village of cottages built of the local Jurassic limestone, which is often of a rich brown or rust colour due to the presence of iron oxide in the rock. And ironically enough, it was the iron deposits that changed Corby into a red brick town and one of the chief industrial centres of the East Midlands. Steam shovels which dug out the ore from open-cast mines at Welford, a little to the east, eventually gave way to the colossal drag-line excavators which cut great scars across the landscape. By about 1950, Corby's steel works had expanded the former village into a place of fifteen thousand inhabitants, and this figure was doubled in the next decade. The works produced a million tons of steel a year. Stewarts and Lloyds, the chief promoters of Corby's growth, imported contingents of Scottish workers, and young men looking for secure jobs came with their wives on the train from Glasgow that came to be called the 'honeymoon express'. It was the so-called Gilchrist-Thomas process that enabled the local phosphoric ore to be used for steel-making by removing its impurities with the addition of lime.

Coventry, West Midlands □   MAP A

Off Foleshill Road, north of the city centre, is a short street called Cash's Lane, named after the Cash brothers, John and Joseph, who built there in 1857 Cash's 'Top Shops'. These brick buildings are on three storeys, the first two being unexceptional Victorian terraced houses arranged round a courtyard, but the floor above them has the characteristic long windows of textile workshops. Cash's considered the houses to be ideal homes at a time when textile workers were suffering hardships everywhere, and machine-breaking had been widespread in the Midlands and the North. Cash's workers did not have to go out to the sound of the factory bell or whistle, but simply went upstairs from home to workshop, and thus kept a little of the independence they prized. This original approach to factory industry did not last long, as the workshops were converted into one factory in the 1860s, but the firm is still in business, in more modern premises, making their famous name-tapes among other things.

Cradley Heath, West Midlands □   MAP A

This district has long specialized in chain-making, and one or two of the original shops still weld wrought-iron chain-links by hand. The chain-making industry is chiefly interesting as an example of the frightful exploitation of labour in the Black Country. The workers at the hot and noisy forges, who included women and children, were cruelly treated in the nineteenth century. They were in metaphorical chains themselves, like slaves, and their lives were awful tales of squalor and misery.

Craigellachie, Grampian +   MAP D

Thomas Telford (*q.v.*) built over a thousand bridges in his native country when he was commissioned to improve communications throughout the Highlands. His bridge across the River Spey at Craigellachie is one of the most notable. Completed in 1815, it is a graceful arched bridge of cast iron with a span of 152 feet between castellated masonry towers. The apparent fragility of the bridge's construction is a tribute to Telford's complete mastery of working with iron.

Cranbrook, Kent ×   MAP A

The Union Mill near the town centre is a fine smock mill in the care of the county council. Built in 1814, it is 72 feet high, and is often said to be the tallest windmill in the country, though that honour properly belongs to a tower mill at Sutton (*q.v.*) in Norfolk. Union Mill has a brick base, white weatherboarding, and an inverted boat-shaped cap. It was built by James Humphrey for the miller Henry Dobell, and is still in working order, though not used.

Craven Arms, Shropshire +   MAP B

An early signpost, pre-dating Telford's improvement of the Holyhead Road in 1811, stands at the junction of the A49 and B4368. It is in the form of a 20-foot high stone obelisk, and gives distances to no less than 36 towns.

Crewe, Cheshire =   MAP B

The railway works at Crewe were built in 1843 for the Grand Junction Railway, which became part of the London and North Western Railway three years later. Terraced housing was built for the imported workers, as there was no existing settlement here when the railway came – only farmland. A population of 5,000 in 1851 had increased to 43,000 by the end of the century, and lines from Chester, Manchester, Liverpool and Birmingham converged on this important junction. The industrial estate was planned by the railway engineer Joseph Locke. Much of the original housing has disappeared, but some survives in Duke Street and its neighbours.

Crich, Derbyshire + MAP B

In the former Crich Cliff Quarry is the Tramway Museum, where tramcars from all parts of Britain and abroad are preserved in working order, with a half-mile track on which a regular service operates with trams decorated with authentic Edwardian advertisements. The museum is on Matlock Road and is open at weekends and bank holidays throughout the year and some weekdays in summer. Tel: Ambergate 2565.

Crinan, Strathclyde ≈ MAP D

The nine-mile-long Crinan Canal was cut through the Kintyre peninsula from Crinan Lock to Loch Fyne to create a passage for shipping that saved a journey of more than a hundred miles. The canal was opened in 1801, and is still a navigable waterway, with locks halfway between the terminal basins at Crinan and Ardrishaig.

Cromford, Derbyshire □ MAP B

The historic site of the first water-powered cotton mill is near the river bridge. The mill was built in 1771 by Richard Arkwright (q.v.), at a time when growing discontent among textile workers was emerging as a threat to machinery, and the austere – not to say grim – building looks like a fortress, though the original mill has been much altered and extended. We are told that there were two hundred employees, 'chiefly children. They work in turns, night and day.' The mill's water power came from the Bonsall Brook and a 'sough' – the stream of an adit made for draining lead mines. Arkwright also built many of the three-storey stone houses in the village for his workers, as well as the church, school and his own home, Willersley Castle, known locally as Arkwright Hall.

Cromford, Derbyshire   □   MAP B

North of the village towards Matlock Bath is Masson Mill, built by Richard Arkwright (*q.v.*) in 1738 as if to prove that nothing succeeds like success. This mill was built of brick instead of stone like the Old Mill in the village, and the original six-storey building survives among the extensions built around it, with Arkwright's peculiar staircase projection with Venetian and small semi-circular windows standing out from the sea of square-headed windows on either side, and with a cupola above. It is altogether a more flamboyant and less forbidding building than the earlier mill. The water-wheel which drove the machinery was fed by a leat at the back of the mill. The building is still in use and not open to the public.

Cromford, Derbyshire   ≈   MAP B

Two miles south-east of the village are an aqueduct and a pumping station connected with the Cromford Canal, promoted by Richard Arkwright (*q.v.*) among others, and built in 1793 by William Jessop. The Wigwell Aqueduct was built of stone to carry the canal over the River Derwent. It has a central span of eighty feet, but the original one collapsed before the canal was opened to traffic, and the company accepted Jessop's offer to pay the £650 cost of rebuilding it. At the north end of the aqueduct is the Leawood Pumping Station, where a beam engine installed in 1849 pumped water from the river to the canal for nearly a hundred years. (It does so no longer.) The unusually elegant stone building has a tall hexagonal chimney. The engine has been restored by the Cromford Canal Society.

Crosthwaite, Cumbria   ☆   MAP B

In the vicinity of the village in the Cartmel Fells, particularly at Mireside, half a mile south, and at Poll Bank Farm, two miles south on minor road to Witherslack, 'spinning galleries' may be observed built into farmhouses. They are wooden galleries beneath extended eaves in seventeenth- and eighteenth-century farmhouses, and were probably designed for storage purposes originally, but were undoubtedly used in summer by the women-folk in their cottage industry of spinning the wool of the local Herdwick sheep with spinning wheel and distaff. Several spinning galleries remain here and there in Cumbria and Lancashire.

D ABRAHAM DARBY

A Quaker ironmaster, Darby was one of the key figures – perhaps *the* key figure – in the rise of modern British industry, having played a vital role in setting the Industrial Revolution in motion. He was born in 1678, the son of a Dudley locksmith, and progressed to iron working through a period as a brass-founder in Bristol. He took over an existing but derelict blast furnace at Coalbrookdale (*q.v.*) which had been set up in 1638, and in 1709 he discovered the method of smelting iron with coke instead of charcoal. Although the process was not widely practised for forty years, the discovery was the crucial step in the mass production of iron for industry, and facilitated the development of the steam engine. Abraham Darby died in 1717, but the family continued their operations in Shropshire through four generations, and it was Abraham Darby III who completed the famous Iron Bridge (*q.v.*) initiated by his father, Abraham II. There is not, as far as I know, any monument to Abraham Darby I anywhere in Britain, although all our lives have been affected by his revolutionary discovery.

Darlington, Durham   =   MAP B

Part of the station at North Road is now a museum devoted to the Stockton and Darlington Railway, the first regular passenger railway, opened in 1825 (although its primary purpose was for freight). Locomotives were used for goods, and passenger trains were pulled by horses at first (on the same tracks). The railway's engineering genius was George Stephenson (*q.v.*) and the financial backing came from a local Quaker businessman, Edward Pease. The inaugural run was done by Stephenson's 'Locomotion', hauling 32 coal wagons at 10 miles an hour, and this historic steam locomotive is now preserved here, among other relics of the pioneering line. Open daily throughout the year except Sunday mornings. Tel: Darlington 460532.

Dartmouth, Devon   ×   MAP A

In Coronation Park is an original Newcomen (*q.v.*) atmospheric engine, which was brought here in 1963 and erected by the Newcomen Society to mark the tri-centenary of the birth of the 'Father of the Steam Engine'. This engine was originally used for pumping water out of the mine workings at Griff Colliery, Nuneaton, from 1723, and was later moved to other sites, ending up at Hawkesbury Junction on the Coventry Canal, where it remained in use until 1913. It is the oldest surviving steam engine.

Delabole, Cornwall △

The old slate quarry here is one of the largest man-made holes in Britain,
and such is the fascination that holes in the ground exercise on the mind of
man that there are special viewing platforms where visitors may stand to
gape at the awesome chasm. Slate has been quarried here since the
fourteenth century, and continuously since at least Tudor times; in those
days there were many separate quarries extracting the valuable material for
use as roofing, flooring, field walls and so on. There was a thriving export
trade in the famous roofing slates of Delabole at one time. In the nineteenth
century the various companies amalgamated and gradually merged their
quarries into this one colossal pit, which has a circumference of about a
mile and a depth of four hundred feet. The slate is still worked but not on
the scale of former times, Welsh slate having monopolized the roofing
market in the Victorian age. Much of the material extracted now is ground
down for various manufacturing purposes, whilst there is a lively trade in
making slate ornaments for the tourist industry.

Derby, Derbyshire ☆

What is thought to have been the first silk mill in England was built here, in
Silk Mill Lane, in 1717. It was rebuilt in 1910 after a disastrous fire, and
now houses the Derby Industrial Museum, where there are exhibits on lead
and coal mining, stone quarrying, textiles and other local industries. The
museum is open from Tuesday to Saturday. Tel: Derby 31111.

Devizes, Wiltshire ≈

Between Devizes and Semington, 8 miles west, the Kennet and Avon
Canal is raised nearly 240 feet by 29 locks. The canal superseded the
Kennet Navigation early in the nineteenth century, linking it with the River
Avon at Bath, so that Somerset coal could be brought east as far as Reading
by water. Seventeen of the locks are grouped closely together at Caen Hill,
west of the town. By the turn of the present century, the canal – owned then
by the Great Western Railway – had become unnavigable, and the locks fell
into dereliction, but much restoration work has been undertaken by
enthusiastic volunteers in recent years.

Devizes, Wiltshire +

West of the town centre on the A361 at the junction with the Chippenham road is a nineteenth-century toll-house, or toll-booth, built in stone like a diminutive castle, with battlements, hoodmoulds and ornamental chimney. It was known locally as Shane's Castle, Shane presumably being the toll-house keeper. It is now a private house, but retains the characteristic features of the Victorian toll-house, with windows facing in both directions (*see* London– Hampstead).

Devoran, Cornwall =   MAP A

Brunel (*q.v.*), though famous for his great works of stone and iron, was also one of the greatest exponents of engineering with timber, and he built many road and rail bridges, particularly in the West Country, using timber beams which could be replaced, when need be, without closing the roads or tracks for long periods. These timber works have all been replaced now, but north-west of Devoran, close to the modern viaduct across the river, are the remaining piers of a timber viaduct Brunel built to carry the Truro–Falmouth branch line of the Great Western Railway.

Digswell, Hertfordshire =   MAP A

At this village near Welwyn Garden City the engineers of the Great Northern Railway found it necessary to build a viaduct to carry the line across the 'impassable barrier' of the little River Mimram, a trickling stream with a valley of soft clay. The viaduct was built by Thomas Brassey to a design by Lewis Cubbitt, using locally made bricks, in 1848–50. It has 40 arches 100 feet high, and is about 1,500 feet in length.

Dinorwic, Gwynedd △   MAP C

This village near Llanberis gave its name to what was once the world's largest slate quarry. The workings ceased in 1969 and the site is now a museum of the industry, open to the public every day during the summer months. There is a fifty-foot waterwheel *in situ*, but demonstrations of machinery and techniques pale beside the awesome sight of the vast quarry itself, extending to an enormous height up the slopes of Elidir Fawr in a great series of terraces. Three thousand men worked here once, producing slates that were shipped all over the world from the specially built Port Dinorwic on the Menai Strait. Tel: Llanberis 630.

Dogdyke, Lincolnshire ✕   MAP B

The Pumping Station at this village on the River Witham near Tattershall was built to drain the surrounding land because shrinkage of the peat (*see* Holme Fen) has left the surface level lower than the rivers. A cast-iron rotative beam engine installed in 1856 remains *in situ*. It drove a scoop wheel of 28 foot diameter which could raise 25 tons of water a minute, and was used until 1940 when a diesel engine and centrifugal pump replaced it, until the station was closed in 1980. It is now preserved by a trust and is open to visitors on the first Sunday of each month from April to October – afternoons only. The station is situated at Bridge Farm, off the A153 west of Tattershall.

Doncaster, South Yorkshire =   MAP B

It was in 1851 that the Great Northern Railway established its locomotive works in Doncaster, and twelve years later the amalgamation of a number of railway companies led to the first regional monopoly, the North Eastern Railway, this business being engineered mainly by George Hudson, the 'Railway King'. By the time of the First World War the company had taken over more than 50 small companies, as well as the docks at Hull (*q.v.*), and its chief locomotive and wagon works at Doncaster employed nearly 5,000 people. Many famous locomotives were built here, especially for the subsequent London and North Eastern Railway. They included 'Flying Scotsman' and 'Mallard', which in 1938 set up the world speed record for a steam locomotive of 126 m.p.h., and which can now be seen at York (*q.v.*).

Dounby, Orkney ✕   MAP D

Click Mill, an old corn mill, north-east of Dounby off the B9057 on Mainland, the largest and chief island of the Orkneys, is a fascinating survival of the type of water mill known as a Norse mill. It has a vertical shaft and a horizontal wheel with inclined wooden blades, and though this system generates little power, it is sufficient to drive a pair of millstones, turning the upper of the two stones as in conventional mills. Still in working order, the mill is maintained as an Ancient Monument by the Department of the Environment.

Dover, Kent ○   MAP A

Within the castle precincts and close to the Saxon church of St Mary-in-

Castro are the remains of a Roman lighthouse, or *pharos*, built early in the imperial occupation of Britain to guide cross-channel vessels. Built of stone rubble faced with ashlar (stone dressed to a smooth finish) and Roman tiles, the original polygonal tower may have been 80 feet high, but it had fallen into ruin by medieval times and was partly rebuilt, probably in the reign of Henry V. It still stands to a height of 40 feet, however, and we can see the original windows which were tiny on the outside walls to prevent draughts interfering with the flames of the beacon at the top. The castle is in the care of the Department of the Environment and can be visited at normal times.

Dudley, West Midlands ☆ MAP A

The Black Country Museum is an open-air complex developed around the site of a group of lime-kilns, near the northern entrance to a tunnel on the Dudley Canal. Lime was used for agricultural purposes and for making cement. Kilns such as these were built for convenience against a hillside so that the raw materials could be fed in from the top and the burnt lime taken out at the bottom. The museum covers canals, mining, and chain-making, among other industries, and is open daily from March to December (except Christmas). Tel: Dudley 9643.

Dufftown, Grampian ▲ MAP D

Scotch whisky is produced at over a hundred distilleries, widely scattered, but the greatest concentration of the industry is along the River Spey and its tributaries. Several companies open their doors to the public, but Grants' Glenfiddich Distillery at Dufftown is singled out here because of its Scotch Whisky Museum. It lies north of the town on the A941. The word 'whisky' comes from the Gaelic 'uisge beatha' – water of life. No one knows when or by whom whisky was invented, but it was being made in Ireland when Henry II carried out his invasion in the twelfth century, and by Tudor times distilling was a thriving industry in Scotland. The special qualities of 'Scotch' depend on drying the barley malt over burning peat, the quality of Scottish water, and the skill of the blenders. It was not until the Spirits Act of 1860 that bottled Scotch whisky could be exported to England. As well as seeing how whisky is made, visitors to the Glenfiddich Distillery can see coopers making oak casks. Open weekdays except winter bank holidays. Tel: Dufftown 375.

Dundee, Tayside ○ MAP D

Whaling and jute were two of the chief sources of Dundee's rise to prominence as a port. The town imported raw jute and from 1832 mixed it with whale oil to produce a material capable of being woven into coarse fabrics such as hessian and sailcloth. In Lower Dens are some fine jute mills built in 1866. The local jute industry employed forty thousand people in the early years of the present century. The Custom House is a neo-classical building of three storeys dating from 1843. Dundee's ship-yards built the polar ships *Terra Nova* and *Discovery*, used by Shackleton and Scott respectively for their Antarctic voyages.

Dundee, Tayside = MAP D

The coming of the railways presented bridge-builders in Scotland with new problems, particularly in crossing the wide estuaries of the Tay and the Forth (*see* South Queensferry). The first Tay Bridge was completed in 1878. It was designed by the prodigious bridge-builder, Thomas Bouch. Twenty men were killed during its construction, but it was the world's longest bridge when completed. The Queen knighted Bouch for his achievement – one of the prides of Victorian engineering. But in the last days of 1879 a frightful storm blew the bridge down as a train was crossing, and 75 more people lost their lives. Sir Thomas Bouch died, a broken man, four months later. It was 8 years before a new bridge was completed beside the remains of the old, the stumps of which can still be seen. The new bridge, designed by W.H. Barlow, was of wrought-iron lattice girder construction, like the old, but proper scientific calculations were made this time to allow for lateral wind pressure – the first time scientific studies of such stresses were made – and the new Tay Bridge, still the longest railway bridge in Britain at just over 2 miles, has stood solid for 100 years, linking Dundee with Fife. It was the last major bridge in Britain to be built of wrought iron.

Dunkeld, Tayside + MAP D

The bridge carrying the A9 across the River Tay is one of the works of Telford (*q.v.*) and is the largest of his masonry bridges, with 7 arches. It was built in 1809. The central arch has a span of 90 feet, flanked by two of 84 feet, then two of 74 feet, the smaller outer arches being of 20-foot span.

Dunston, Tyne & Wear ○ MAP B

Timber staithes remain at this port on the River Tyne, some of the last such structures built in the nineteenth century as wharves for unloading coal from the railway on to waiting ships.

Dutton, Cheshire = MAP B

The stone railway viaduct crossing the valley of the River Weaver dates from 1837, and was built by George Stephenson (*q.v.*) and Joseph Locke, for the Grand Junction Railway. It has 20 arches of 60-foot span.

Earith, Cambridgeshire ▲ MAP A

From this Fenland village the Old and New Bedford Rivers take off north-eastward, straight as arrows, to join the Ouse near Downham Market. These canals were dug in the seventeenth century (in 1630 and 1650) as part of the great engineering work undertaken by the Earl of Bedford to reclaim valuable agricultural land from the sea. Cornelius Vermuyden was the Dutch expert employed by the earl and his 'co-adventurers', as the promoters of the scheme called themselves. Vermuyden constructed the first Bedford River, twenty-one miles long, to drain the so-called Bedford Level, and it was highly effective for a time, but the one factor the engineer failed to foresee was that the dried-out land would shrink (*see* Holme Fen), and soon the level of the canal was above that of the surrounding land. A partial answer to this problem was the building of hundreds of windmills to pump water back into the specially constructed drainage channels, and these were succeeded by steam pumps (*see* Stretham). These great works, at any rate, converted shallow waters, where 'fen slodgers' had fished for eels and caught waterfowl for the town markets, into the most fertile soil in Britain, where rich harvests are now reaped.

East Bergholt, Suffolk ▲ MAP A

The large weatherboarded mill on the River Stour a mile and a half to the south-east of the village is Flatford Mill, the former home of John Constable, whose father was a prosperous miller. The National Trust owns it now, but it is not open to the public as it is rented to the Council for the Promotion of Field Studies. One immediately recognizes the building from Constable's many paintings of it. It is a substantial brick watermill, and dates from the seventeenth century.

Eastbourne, East Sussex ☆ MAP A

The lighthouse beneath the cliffs at Beachy Head, three miles south-west of the town, replaced an earlier clifftop lighthouse farther west, built in 1831 by Thomas Stevenson, father of the author of *Treasure Island* (*see also* Girdle Ness). The castle-like old lighthouse, built of Aberdeen granite, has lost its lantern housing, and is now a private dwelling.

East Linton, Lothian ✕ MAP D

Preston Mill was built in the middle of the eighteenth century as a corn mill powered by a cast-iron waterwheel driven from a large millpond. It is an attractive low rubble-stone building with pantile roof, and has a conical drying kiln alongside the grinding mill. The Scottish millwright and inventor Andrew Meikle worked on the mill, which is the oldest water-driven grain mill surviving in Scotland. It is owned by the Scottish National Trust, and is open to visitors every day except Sunday mornings through-out the year. The mill stands north-east of the village beside the river.

Easton, Suffolk ▲ MAP A

The Easton Farm Park is a private working farm and museum, the original farm itself dating from the 1870s, when it was built as a model dairy farm by the Duke of Hamilton. The Victorian buildings display tools and machin-ery of the period, and redundant breeds of farm animals are preserved here. The farm is open daily during the summer months. Tel: Wickham Market 746475.

Eccles, Greater Manchester ≈ MAP B

South-west of the town, Barton Swing Aqueduct, built in 1894, replaced the masonry aqueduct built by James Brindley (*q.v.*) to carry the Bridgewa-ter Canal over the Irwell valley. The new aqueduct was necessary to allow ships to pass on the new Manchester Ship Canal. It was designed by Sir E. Leader Williams, the ship canal's engineer, and is a colossal steel tank, 78 yards long and weighing 1,450 tons, pivoted in the middle to swing through 90° by hydraulic power when required. If Brindley's detractors thought his stone aqueduct was a mad idea, it is as well they were not alive to see this amazing piece of engineering successfully accomplished.

Opposite
*Preston Water
Mill at East
Linton*

Eccles, Greater Manchester ☆   MAP B

In Wellington Road is Monks Hall Museum, where an interesting collection of industrial machinery is on display – in particular machines invented
by James Nasmyth, the Scottish engineer who set up his works in Manchester. The steam hammer seen here was his best known work. It was
raised vertically by steam pressure and allowed to fall by its own weight.
The museum is open every day except Sunday. Tel: Manchester 789-
4372.

Edinburgh, Lothian ☆   MAP D

The Royal Scottish Museum in Chambers Street has many industrial
exhibits, including sections on mining, shipping and transport. Open daily
throughout the year except Sunday mornings. Tel: Edinburgh 225 7534.

Eling, Hampshire ✕   MAP A

The Eling tide mill, south of Totton at the mouth of Bartley Water, is an
eighteenth-century brick mill with two waterwheels driving its machinery.
The original mill here was built in the eleventh century. Although abandoned as derelict in the early 1960s, the present building has now been
restored and is open as a working museum, producing stone-ground flour
for sale. It is said to be the only tide mill in western Europe that is still
operating. Tide mills were built in coastal districts to take advantage of high
tides, when water was impounded in a mill pond, to be used to power the
waterwheels at low water. Working hours were thus dictated by tides, and
the mill can only operate at favourable times. The causeway near the mill,
crossing the creek, is a toll bridge, with tollbooth intact.

Ellesmere Port, Cheshire ≈   MAP B

The port was created in 1795 when Thomas Telford (*q.v.*) brought the
Ellesmere Canal from Chester and made a tidal basin (1801). Later he
built a series of fine warehouses and laid out a dock estate. After his death,
William Cubitt continued the development, and further industrial promotion came with the building of the Manchester Ship Canal at the end of the
nineteenth century. Telford's warehouses were mostly destroyed by fire in
1970, but Porters Row survives as an example of his workers' houses, and

locks on what is now the Shropshire Union Canal descend the hillside to link it with the ship canal. In Dock Yard Road, a Boat Museum houses the country's largest collection of inland waterway vessels, many of which can be inspected by visitors. The museum is open every day from Easter to October. Tel: Liverpool 355 1876.

Elsecar, South Yorkshire   ✕   MAP B

Elsecar is a mining village south of Barnsley, and has some interesting buildings of the nineteenth century around the former iron works, but it is especially noted for the unique pumping engine preserved by the National Coal Board. It is the oldest Newcomen-type steam engine surviving in Britain on its original site, having been installed in 1787 to drain the colliery, and it remained in use until 1923. Some alterations have been made to it, such as substituting a cast-iron beam for the original timber one, but it is basically intact as built, and interested visitors can see it on application to the Coal Board's local area office.

Boat Museum at Ellesmere Port

Elterwater, Cumbria   ☐   MAP B

The village was an important source of gunpowder in the nineteenth

century, and remains of the industry can still be seen. The mill was sited on the B5343, and was in operation from 1824 until 1928. The industry grew up in the Lake District because there was a demand for gunpowder in the slate quarries and copper mines of the region, and because of the ready availability of birch and alder for charcoal and fast flowing becks to drive the machinery in the area. Added to this was the important fact that the works could be sited in remote places for safety, for the making of gunpowder was a dangerous business. There were occasional accidental explosions and several deaths during the century of the mill's existence. Workmen wore special boots made without nails, and horses used for haulage were shod with copper rather than iron, in order to reduce the risk from flying sparks. Saltpetre was imported from India and sulphur from Italy, and brought to the Lake District gunpowder works by water from Liverpool to Milnthorpe.

Exeter, Devon ☆   MAP A

The Exeter Maritime Museum is located in the former Victorian warehouses alongside the Exeter Ship Canal, built to allow vessels of 400 tons to reach the city centre from the estuary of the River Exe. There has been a navigable waterway to Exeter, in fact, since the sixteenth century. There is a brick-built two-storey Customs House, built in 1681, and the museum itself contains boats of all kinds from many parts of the world. Open daily. Tel: Exeter 58075.

Exeter, Devon ☆   MAP A

Beneath the city streets is a network of passages which were made as aqueducts in the thirteenth century, to carry water from local springs into the medieval walled town. Some of the passages can be explored, and are accessible from Princesshay, parallel with the High Street. Open during afternoons from Tuesday to Saturday throughout the year.

Fairburn, North Yorkshire +   MAP B

Fairburn had a busy quarrying industry at one time, and to provide transportation of the stone from the quarries to the River Aire a tramway was constructed early in the nineteenth century to link up with a short section of canal to the river. Parts of the tramway rails can be traced as well as a tunnel.

Falkirk, Central   =   MAP D

In Wallace Street is the museum of the Scottish Railways Preservation
Society, with a good collection of locomotives and rolling stock. Open on
Saturdays when locomotives are occasionally in steam.

Fareham, Hampshire   □   MAP A

Two and a half miles north-west of the town centre by the River Meon is
the site of the Funtley Iron Mill, an eighteenth-century forge where Henry
Cort, whose house remains nearby, developed in 1784 the 'dry puddling'
process for producing wrought iron on a large scale. Molten pig iron heated
by coal in a reverbatory furnace was purified into 'malleable' iron by the air
circulating through the furnace. The discovery led to the migration of iron
works from the small forges of the south-east and elsewhere to the
coalfields of the Midlands and the north, because it became a mass-
production industry.

Faversham, Kent   □   MAP A

For three hundred years, until around 1934, Faversham was a major centre
of gunpowder manufacture, and one of the former factories, Chart Mills,
was saved from demolition in recent years by the Faversham Society, when
the area in which it stands was being cleared for a new housing estate. The
mill has become the subject of a thorough restoration programme. The mill
was powered by water and became part of the Royal Powder Mill in the
eighteenth century. It stands on the west bank of the River Swale, half a
mile from the town centre. The building, which was originally one of four
mills, dates from the 1760s, and is the oldest of its kind in the world. Open
on bank holiday afternoons or by previous arrangement. Tel: Faversham
4542.

Fenton, Staffordshire   □   MAP B (*Stoke-on-Trent*)

There is little to see of the Potteries at Fenton other than relatively modern
factories, but a couple of bottle ovens, now rather rare (*see* Longton) survive
near King Street. Old photographs of the Potteries show a jungle of bottle
ovens seen only dimly through the permanent pall of smoke that was
rivalled in its denseness at one time only by Sheffield and the Black
Country.

Finsthwaite, Cumbria □   MAP B

Near this village at the southern end of Windermere is Stott Park, where a nineteenth-century bobbin mill is preserved by the Department of the Environment, complete with its barns, lathes and a small horizontal steam engine used before electricity was installed. This mill remained in operation until 1971, but the introduction of plastic bobbins killed off this local coppice industry (*see* Caldbeck) which shared the fortunes of the cotton industry in Lancashire. The barns were used for storing timber ready for use in the mills. (The processes of making the holes in the bobbins, which had to be to exact specifications, was called 'wrincing'.) This mill is open to the public.

Flamborough Head, Humberside ○   MAP B

The end of the road to Flamborough Head brings one to the octagonal old lighthouse, built of stone in 1674 by Sir John Clayton. It was replaced in 1806 by John Matson's new lighthouse a short distance away, but still stands to its original four-storey height and is the only complete coal-burning lighthouse left in the country. It is thought that the Romans were first to erect a beacon light on this treacherous stretch of coast where many ships have foundered.

Fourstones, Northumberland ▲   MAP B

Threshing machinery was driven by horse-wheel when mechanical threshing was introduced from Scotland late in the eighteenth century with the development of the threshing drum, to relieve men from the real hard labour of threshing with flails, although in areas where the straw was required for thatching, hand-threshing continued long after the appearance of machinery. Several horse-wheels survive in Northumberland, housed in circular buildings with their roofs supported by pillars of timber or stone. At Fourstones, north-east of Haydon Bridge, a wheel house adjoins the engine house built to replace it when steam engines came into use for threshing. By this time in Durham one J. Bailey (no relation) had written that 'the expense of horses is now become so great, that they should not be used where it can be avoided. Water, where it can be obtained, is certainly the cheapest. Wind, tho' an uncertain power, is in many instances used; but in this county, where coals are so cheap, and in most cases at no great distance, steam is probably the best and most effective power that can be employed . . .'

Foxton, Leicestershire ≈ MAP A

The so-called 'Foxton Staircase' is a remarkable set of ten locks on the Grand Union Canal. When the Leicestershire and Northamptonshire Union Canal was being constructed to link the River Trent with the Grand Junction Canal at Northampton, and thus with London, work came to a halt at Gumley due to disputes about the proposed route and the high cost of constructing a tunnel through the hillside between Gumley and Foxton. When the newly formed Grand Union Canal Company resumed work in 1810, Thomas Telford (*q.v.*) suggested the construction of a set of locks instead of the tunnel. The locks were built in 2 staircases of 5, and were regarded as one of the great engineering achievements of the age. They lifted the canal over the hill, raising the water level by 75 feet. Forty thousand tons of traffic a year passed through the locks at the height of their commercial usage. A narrow boat and butty took over three-quarters of an hour to negotiate the locks, however, and an inclined plane was eventually built to speed up traffic by lifting boats in movable docks. This was not wholly successful and was soon abandoned. The concrete ramps are still there, hidden in the undergrowth.

Furnace, Dyfed □ MAP C

It is no surprise to learn that this village got its name from the local industries of smelting silver and iron. A blast furnace was set up here in 1755 by Jonathan Kendall, powered by a waterwheel and fired with charcoal, and it remains *in situ* beside the River Dovey, the subject of preservation for public interest.

Gateshead, Tyne & Wear △ MAP B

The large engine house built for a pumping engine at Friars Goose colliery has been preserved here by the local authority. It is a stone-built structure of the early nineteenth century, and stands overlooking the river east of the town centre.

Gilfach Goch, Mid-Glamorgan △ MAP C

At this village near Tonyrefail visitors can follow a two-mile-long Industrial Trail through the countryside that inspired Richard Llewellyn's famous 1939 novel *How Green was My Valley*. A century of coal-mining activity had made a depressing scene of this valley until imaginative landscaping during the last two decades transformed it. The trail begins at the north end of the village.

Girdle Ness, Grampian ○   MAP D

The lighthouse on this headland south-east of Aberdeen was built in the 1830s to the design of Robert Stevenson. (Not to be confused with Stephenson the railway engineer! This one was the grandfather of Robert Louis Stevenson, who was himself intended to be a lighthouse engineer like his grandfather, his father and his uncle, until circumstances made him an author instead.) The lighthouse can be visited at certain times, at the keeper's convenience. The Bell Rock lighthouse off Arbroath was another of Stevenson's works.

Glan Conwy, Gwynedd ×   MAP C

The Felin Isaf corn mill is a stone-built water mill built around 1730. It worked regularly for over a hundred and fifty years, its machinery driven by an undershot wheel which remains. The mill has been restored to full working order and grinds wholemeal flour. It is open every day except Monday in the summer months (afternoons only on Sundays). Tel: Glan Conwy 646.

Glasgow, Strathclyde =   MAP D

The city's Central Station incorporates a large viaduct section over Argyll Street, which is locally nicknamed the Highlandman's Umbrella, because it provided useful shelter for the homeless and unemployed in the city.

Glasgow, Strathclyde ☆   MAP D

The Museum of Transport in Albert Drive has an interesting collection of trams and steam locomotives, among other forms of transport. It is open every day except Sunday mornings. Tel: Glasgow 423 8000.

Glasgow, Strathclyde ☆   MAP D

What was formerly the West Street Cotton Company's factory – now the Templeton Carpets factory – is a piece of Victorian eccentricity in industrial building almost without rival, except possibly for Marshall's Mill in Leeds (*q.v.*). It was built in Arabian style, with multi-coloured bricks and inlaid tiles, Arabian arches and a staircase tower like a Moslem minaret. Anything less like a cotton mill would be hard to find, and if only Templetons made flying carpets, it would be perfect.

Glenfield, Leicestershire   =   MAP A

The blocked-up western entrance to the Glenfield Tunnel is the only remnant of the Leicester and Swannington Railway, the first line in the Midlands, opened in 1832. It was built by the Stephensons (*q.v.*) and John Ellis, who succeeded the formidable George Hudson as Chairman of the Midland Railway Company. Ellis and Robert Stephenson both had mining interests in the Leicestershire coalfield, and the purpose of the railway was to convey coal into Leicester by faster and more direct means than by canal barge. The tunnel was the longest in Britain at the time, the first over a mile in length. The first locomotive to run on the line was the 'Comet', brought by canal for the occasion and driven by George Stephenson himself, to the sound of a band and a salute of cannon fire. Necessity being the mother of invention, a collision between an engine named 'Samson' and a cartload of butter and eggs led to the use on this line of the first train whistle, made by a local organbuilder.

Glenfinnan, Highland   =   MAP D

The viaduct carrying the Mallaig section of the West Highland Railway round the head of Loch Shiel is one of the few railway viaducts to be built of concrete. The long curving bridge has 21 arches with spans of 50 feet, and was completed in 1898.

Gloucester, Gloucestershire   ○   MAP A

Gloucester's modern docks were created in 1827 with the building of the Gloucester and Berkeley Ship Canal, which allowed vessels of 750 tons to reach the city by avoiding the dangers of the Severn estuary. Today the docks are little used except by barges carrying timber, but they cover an area of eight acres and many elegant brick-built warehouses and wharves survive. Of particular interest is the Pillar Warehouse of 1849, a four-storey building with a Doric colonnade of cast-iron columns facing the quayside. Telford (*q.v.*) had a considerable hand in this canal project in his old age, but the chief engineer was Robert Mylne.

Goathland, North Yorkshire   =   MAP B

The horse-drawn Whitby and Pickering Railway of George Stephenson (*q.v.*) required the building of the Moorgate bridge in 1835, a few miles south of this village on the North York Moors. It is a stone bridge which was abandoned within twelve years when the railway was re-aligned for steam locomotive operation.

Goole, Humberside   ○   MAP B

The port of Goole on the River Ouse was opened in 1826, at the junction of the Aire and Calder Navigation with the Ouse and the Don, and became an important Victorian canal port, providing a link with the Humber and the North Sea for places such as Doncaster, Wakefield and Sheffield. (Goole was then in the West Riding of Yorkshire.) The chief cargo handled here was coal, and within a century the population of Goole had shot up from under 500 to 20,000 The docks are close to the centre of the town, which was largely the creation of the canal company that built the docks with their brick warehouses and harbour offices. The collapse of the export market for Yorkshire coal brought about the decline of the port.

Grangemouth, Central   ○   MAP D

The port at Grangemouth was opened in 1777 to take advantage of trade resulting from the construction of the Forth and Clyde Canal. The canal is now disused and partly filled in, but its course can be followed, and it has the remains of locks, aqueducts and a tunnel. The canal was begun by John Smeaton, and completed in 1790 by Robert Whitworth. Both James Watt and Thomas Telford (*qq.v.*) were consulted in the course of the canal's construction. It brought mainly coal and chemicals to the port for shipping to the Continent.

Grassington, North Yorkshire   △   MAP B

Extensive lead mining was done on Grassington Moor, north-east of this Wharfedale village, from at least as early as the Tudor period, and some remains of the industry are still to be seen, mainly dating from the eighteenth and nineteenth centuries. One of the main problems here was lack of water for washing the ore, and by the early nineteenth century the Duke of Devonshire, who owned the workings, had built a watercourse and an underground drainage channel to allow deeper shafts to be sunk. The watercourse, known as the Duke's Level, eventually drove waterwheels for the mechanical dressing of the ore. The chimney of the so-called New Mill, built in 1850 and no longer in use, is the most prominent sign of the local industry, with a long flue rising up the hillside from the smelting furnaces some distance away. The reason for such a long flue, which is not uncommon, is that vapours given off during smelting of lead polluted the surrounding landscape, whereas long flues allowed the fumes to settle harmlessly. Some Pennine lead flues were up to two miles long.

Great Amwell, Hertfordshire ≈   MAP A

On a little island in the river at this attractive village is a small stone monument to Sir Hugh Myddelton, a wealthy mine-owner and Member of Parliament, who constructed an artificial waterway in 1613 to carry much-needed drinking water to London from springs here and at Chadwell. The waterway was called the New River, and it originally ran forty miles to Clerkenwell. Myddelton carried out the work at his own expense, but the city corporation was responsible for building and maintaining bridges 'for the passage of the King's subjects over the said river or cut'. The oldest surviving bridge is an iron one built in 1824 to carry a by-road across the New River from the A10 to Great Amwell village. New River Company shares were worth a fortune in the nineteenth century.

Great Bardfield, Essex ×   MAP A

The windmill at the eastern approach to the village is known as Gibraltar Mill, and has undergone many transformations in the course of its life, from its original construction in 1680 to its recent conversion to a private house. It is said to have been built as a smock mill but later, after a period as a dwelling house, changed to a tower mill and made higher.

Great Bedwyn, Wiltshire ≈   MAP A

Between this village and the A346 to the west is the Crofton Pumping Station, a three-storey brick building at the summit of the Kennet and Avon Canal. It was built to pump water forty feet up from Wilton Water, as the canal is much higher at this point than the source of the River Kennet. The pumps were operated by two Cornish beam engines supplied by Boulton and Watt and Harveys of Hayle in 1812 and 1846 respectively. The Boulton and Watt job, with its huge cast-iron beam, is reckoned to be the world's oldest engine still running on steam. The Kennet and Avon Canal Trust preserves the engines, which can be seen on Sundays and are occasionally in steam.

Great Coxwell, Oxfordshire ▲ MAP A

The great thirteenth-century tithe barn, built of stone quarried near the site, was originally the property of Beaulieu Abbey, which was granted the manor of Faringdon by King John. It stands 50 feet high and over 50 yards long. Stone buttresses reinforce the roughly coursed walls, and the roof is of graded courses of Stonesfield stone tiles, borne on massive beams, bracing struts and oak posts on 7-foot high stone bases. Tithe barns were built by the Church for the exploitation of peasant labour, the peasants being obliged to submit to the Church one tenth of all they produced. This barn is owned by the National Trust, and is open throughout the year.

Great Yarmouth, Norfolk ☆ MAP A

At Haven Bridge, crossing the River Yare near the Town Hall, is a rare surviving example of a commercial ice-house. Ice-houses in Britain date from the seventeenth century, and many of the great houses had private ice-houses built in their grounds before the advent of refrigeration – some were still used well into the present century. Holes in the ground for preserving ice were known in Italy in 1580, and Sir Francis Bacon died from a chill in 1626 after testing his theory that stuffing a chicken with ice would preserve it. The essential properties of an ice-house were a cool dry place – usually but not always underground – with insulation from the sun's heat and good drainage. A thick thatch was often used in Italy to keep the interior cool, and the ice-house at Yarmouth has a thatched roof. The upper part of such buildings, where the entrance was above ground, was often used as a cold store, with ice preserved below in a kind of cellar, on a bed of straw which provided the necessary drainage.

Greenhow, North Yorkshire △ MAP B

Like nearby Grassington (*q.v.*), the village was involved in exploitation of mineral deposits beneath the moors to the north, and there are ruins of eighteenth-and nineteenth-century smelt mills as well as the so-called 'Panty Oon Stone' – a hollowed-out stone thought to have been used by medieval lead miners for dressing the ore.

Greenock, Strathclyde ☆ MAP D

As well as a section on the local shipbuilding industry, the McLean Museum in Union Street has important exhibits connected with the steam-engine pioneer James Watt (*q.v.*), who was born in the town, and who was involved in the improvement of the harbours here and at Port Glasgow. The museum is open on weekdays throughout the year. Tel: Greenock 23741.

Grimsby, Humberside   ○   MAP B

The notable landmark at Grimsby Docks is a 313-foot high brick tower standing between the entrance locks. It was built in 1852 by J.W. Wild, who modelled it – if you please – on the tower of the town hall in Siena; its purpose was to provide the docks with their own hydraulic power, having a huge tank of water pumped up by a steam engine. Wild built the tower for the Manchester, Sheffield and Lincolnshire Railway, which had merged with the Grimsby Docks Company and brought the railway here in 1848. It is now used as a television relay station and as a sluice for the Fish Dock (*q.v.*).

Grimsby, Humberside   ▲   MAP B

Grimsby's Fish Dock is said to the the world's biggest fish market, with nearly a mile of quays. Fishing was Grimsby's *raison d'être* as long ago as the thirteenth century, and it is the oldest chartered (i.e. granted written rights and privileges by the king) town in England. Cod, plaice, sole and turbot have long been the chief catches in the deep-sea fishing grounds of the North Sea, and the trawler, with which Grimsby's name is synonymous, was introduced in the nineteenth century to drag a wide-mouthed net along the sea floor, to catch these so-called 'ground fish'. Steam power and storage of their catches in ice were among the developments that brought increased efficiency to the trawler fleets, but the fleet – once Britain's largest – has been depleted because of over-fishing and the 'Cod Wars' with Iceland.

Grosmont, North Yorkshire   =   MAP B

A tunnel taking a footpath through a hillside close to the village church was actually built in 1835 for Stephenson's (*q.v.*) horse-drawn Whitby and Pickering Railway. At the northern end of the hundred-yard tunnel former stables for the horses survive. Parallel with this tunnel is the more modern railway tunnel, though 'more modern' only by twelve years and the substitution of a steam locomotive for horsepower. The old tunnel is now as silent as the 's' in Grosmont.

Gwennap, Cornwall ☆   MAP A

Two miles to the north-west of this village near Redruth in the desolate
former tin-mining region of Cornwall is Gwennap Pit which, although not
exactly an industrial monument, has great significance in the social history
of the local tinners, who were often ruthlessly exploited by their employers
and were obvious targets for the message of Nonconformism. Gwennap Pit
was originally an amphitheatre created by mining subsidence, and it is said
that tinners held their cock-fighting 'mains' (matches) in it, but in the
eighteenth century John Wesley preached his fiery sermons to the large
crowds of tinners and their families who gathered here. It was eventually
terraced and became known as a sort of Methodist 'cathedral'. Visitors can
see it at any time. A service is still held here by Methodists every Whit
Sunday.

Haigh, Greater Manchester △   MAP B

In Haigh Park there is an industrial trail incorporating coal-mining
remains, and including the re-erected winding gear of a local pit, and the
scene of illicit open-cast mining during the 1926 General Strike. There are
also signs of early glass works and mine railways, but the chief monument
here is the Great Haigh Sough, begun by Sir Roger Bradshaigh in 1652 to
drain water from his mines, and one of the oldest such systems in the area.
The tunnel was extended in the nineteenth century, and is over a thousand
yards long.

Halifax, West Yorkshire ☆   MAP B

The Piece Hall in Thomas Street is the only surviving example of an
eighteenth-century cloth market. Built in 1775–9 round a large quadrang-
le, the hall is on two and three storeys with continuous colonnades, and
consists of more than three hundred separate rooms or offices where cloth
makers displayed their wares to the wholesale merchants on Saturday
mornings. After being degraded to the level of a vegetable market, the
Piece Hall was rightly recognized as an architectural and industrial
monument that it was important to preserve, and part of it now houses the
town's Textile Museum, which is open throughout the year. Tel: Halifax
59031.

Halifax, West Yorkshire ☆   MAP B

In Skircoat Moor Road is a slender octagonal tower 253 feet high which
was built in 1875 as a chimney for the dye-works of J.E. Wainhouse. It is of
flamboyant design, and is locally known as Wainhouse Tower.

Hallsands, Devon ☆   MAP A

Below the cliffs at this lonely coastal village are the ruined granite houses of
the original village of Hallsands, once a thriving place chiefly occupied in
crab fishing. Its houses, shop, pub and post office were built on a narrow
shelf of rock looking out over Start Bay, and it had a population of more
than a hundred people. At the end of the nineteenth century, dredging for
gravel began in the bay when extensions to Devonport's naval dockyard
were planned, and the sinking of the protective shingle beach left Hallsands exposed to the winter storms, which in 1917 were so severe that after
two days only one house was left standing. Some compensation was
eventually paid to the villagers by the Board of Trade, after much
prevarication and talk of 'natural causes'; the fact was the Board had
permitted the dredging operation without foreseeing the consequences. A
new community grew up on the safer site at the top of the cliffs.

Hamsterley, Durham ☐   MAP B

North-west of the village at Derwentcote are the remains of a cementation
furnace dating from the early eighteenth century, a rare survival. Built of
stone and of conical shape, it was used to make steel by heating wrought
iron with charcoal in sealed fireclay pots, so that the high carbon content of
the charcoal was absorbed by the molten metal and became steel. The
furnace is scheduled as an Ancient Monument in the care of the Department of the Environment, and can be seen at any time.

Hanley, Staffordshire ☐   MAP B *(Stoke-on-Trent)*

Etruria, the model village build by Josiah Wedgwood (*q.v.*) for the workers in
his pottery factory, stood beside the Trent and Mersey Canal at Hanley. But
when Wedgwoods moved the Barlaston before the Second World War, the
place became a steel works, and all the old buildings and kilns have since
been demolished by the British Steel Corporation. Near the summit locks on
the canal, however, is a preserved building called the Etruscan Bone and
Flint Mill, which was built in 1857 to process raw materials for the potteries.

Harbury, Warwickshire   ×   MAP A

The Chesterton windmill, between this village and Chesterton Green, is
certainly the oddest looking in Britain, notwithstanding the multi-sailed
windmills to be seen in Lincolnshire. Technically it is a tower mill, with the
sails mounted on a rotatable cap. But instead of rising solidly from ground
level, the mill is supported on stone arches. It was built in 1632 by Sir
Edward Peyto, some say to a design by Inigo Jones, though that is
unproven. Whoever designed it intended it to be an eye-catcher as well as a
practical building, and it remains a local landmark in the middle of a field,
Peyto's estate having long gone. There is no way up to the upper floor. A
ladder must have been used to gain access when the mill was in use.

Harrold, Bedfordshire   □   MAP A

Before the Industrial Revolution, many villages in Bedfordshire, Hertfordshire and Buckinghamshire had a thriving cottage industry in hand

lace-making. Few visible signs of such domestic industries remain, but the fine octagonal market house on the village green at Harrold is where work was distributed among the lace-makers, and where they brought the finished lace to be paid for by the employers.

Hartington, Derbyshire   =   MAP B

A short tunnel was built east of the village in 1825 to take the Cromford and High Peak Railway under the main road between Ashbourne and Buxton (A515). The railway company's coat of arms is on the western portal of local stone, while a plaque at the other end records the name of the engineer who built it, Josiah Jessop.

Harwich, Essex   ○   MAP A

On the green, not far from the town centre, is a weatherboarded shed with pantile roof, fenced in, which houses a crane from the old naval dockyard. It was removed to the present site in 1928, but was originally built in the second half of the seventeenth century. It may well be the oldest crane in Britain, and it was operated by men on treadwheels. There are two wheels of 16-foot diameter, and the 18-foot jib could swing through 180°.

Hastings, East Sussex   ☆   MAP A

East of the town beyond the harbour area are the most interesting buildings in Hastings, the weatherboarded net stores or lofts, locally known as 'deezes'. They are tall buildings of varying height, with saddleback roofs, and coated with tar. Unique to Hastings, they were built tall on concrete bases to save the fishermen ground rent on stores with enough space for their nets. Their style seems Scandinavian, and although some were rebuilt after a fire, this type of building has remained in use here since the sixteenth century for storing nets and other equipment.

Hathersage, Derbyshire   □   MAP B

Where the A625 road from Hathersage to Sheffield crosses one of the 'edges' peculiar to the Peak District, just before reaching the Yorkshire border, the keen explorer may find heaps of unfinished millstones in the undergrowth. The 'edges' are an almost continuous series of jagged scarps or outcrops where the hard carboniferous sandstone juts out from the softer rock which has been worn away by the elements over millions of years. Carboniferous sandstone is also known as Millstone Grit, and this particular 'edge' is called Millstone Edge. There was a thriving industry in this area once, supplying millstones and grindstones to all parts of Britain and across the world. The grindstones went especially to the steel works of Sheffield (*q.v.*). In and around the long-abandoned quarries are millstones which the workers had barely started on; others with their circular shapes and central holes; a few even have the radial grooves or 'harps' chiselled into them, ready for use in the flour mills; but all left lying when the trade collapsed under competition in the eighteenth century from imported French Burr stones, which were thought to be of better quality for the purpose. These stones were even harder than Millstone Grit, and were often used for grinding wheat, while the Derbyshire stone was retained for oats and barley. The local industry was centuries old, but has disappeared almost without trace, and so excites little interest among 'industrial archaeologists'.

Haverfordwest, Dyfed   ○   MAP C

The town, standing on the Western Cleddau, which is navigable this far, became a prosperous port in the eighteenth century, and in Quay Street, on the river's west bank, several warehouses of the period are preserved.

Hawick, Borders   □   MAP D

Hawick is one of the main centres of Scotland's textile industry, with mills established to take advantage of the power provided by local streams and rivers. Trow Mill stands in a picturesque site two miles north-east of the town on the A698. Tweeds and blankets are woven here, and visitors can see all the machinery and processes involved. The mill is open on working days throughout the year. Tel: Hawick 2555.

Haworth, West Yorkshire   =   MAP B

The village or small town most famous and most visited as the home of the Brontë family seems an unlikely destination for railway enthusiasts, but at Haworth station the preserved Keighley and Worth Valley Railway has its headquarters and museum, where there is a collection of locomotives and rolling stock. The line featured in the film *The Railway Children*. Trains are operated on the line at weekends, between Keighley and Oxenhope. The museum is open daily.

Hayle, Cornwall □ MAP A

The site of Harveys' Foundry in Foundry Square is an historic spot in industrial terms. Opened in 1779 by the village blacksmith, John Harvey, it was soon building some of the world's largest boilers and stationary steam engines. Richard Trevithick (*q.v.*) was John Harvey's son-in-law, and the firm exploited Trevithick's pioneering engine designs.

Haytor Down, Devon △ MAP A

Four miles west of Bovey Tracey, on the east side of Dartmoor, are the abandoned granite quarries of Haytor, opened early in the nineteenth century by George Templer. Some say the stone from these quarries was the hardest of the Dartmoor granites. At any rate, Templer won a contract to supply granite for the new London Bridge, built in 1825–31 to replace the earlier one which was no longer safe or adequate. To facilitate the efficient transport of granite from his quarries to the waiting canal barges at Teigngrace, Templer built a tramway, using long shaped blocks of his own granite to form the rails. Teams of horses in single file hauled trains of a dozen flat-topped wagons loaded with granite along these rails. Over a quarter of a million tons were supplied for London Bridge. The tramway remained in operation for forty years, during which time the Haytor quarries also supplied granite for the British Museum and many other famous buildings. The tramway was finally abandoned in 1858, but parts of it remain *in situ*, overgrown with grass and weeds, near the Manaton road.

Helmshore, Lancashire □ MAP B

At this village near Haslingden is the Higher Mill Museum, originally a water-powered fulling mill built in 1789. Five pairs of nineteenth-century fulling stocks are preserved here, as well as the eighteen-foot breastshot waterwheel and a rotative beam engine. In an adjoining spinning mill there is a fine collection of early spinning machinery and power looms. Open every afternoon from March to November. Tel: Rossendale 26459.

Henfield, West Sussex × MAP A

Woods Hill, on the A2037 south of the village, is a four-storey corn mill partly of brick and stone, partly timber-framed and weatherboarded, on a tributary stream of the River Adur. Powered by an overshot iron water-wheel, the mill ceased commercial operation in 1927 and now belongs to

the Sussex Trust for Nature Conservation. It is open on summer afternoons except Mondays and Fridays. Tel: Henfield 2630.

Henley, Somerset ▲   MAP A

North-east of the village the River Cary becomes the King's Sedgemoor
Drain, chief of the artificial 'rhines' or watercourses cut to drain the
Somerset Levels, which lie below sea level. King's Sedgemoor Drain, cut
at the end of the eighteenth century, runs as straight as an arrow across the
marshy landscape to carry surplus water to the River Parrett. The canal
engineer William Jessop was largely responsible for this pioneering work
which had been in prospect ever since the Stuart period.

Heptonstall, West Yorkshire ☆   MAP B

A remarkable industrial contrast can be seen between this stone-built
weaving village up on the moors and Hebden Bridge in the valley below it.
A vernacular sign heralds one's arrival at 'Top oth town' in Heptonstall,
where 'Weavers Square' stands as witness to the age-old cottage preoc-
cupation of the villagers with hand-loom weaving. There are many cottages
with long mullioned windows on the upper floors. When factory industry
began to take over, however, the mills were built at Hebden Bridge below,
to take advantage of the water-power provided by the river and the
transport facility of the canal, so Hebden Bridge grew fast into a busy mill
town whilst Heptonstall remained as it had always been. It is also worth
noting that, whereas the mills of the Lancashire cotton trade on the west
side of the Pennines are mostly of brick, the wool mills of Yorkshire, on the
east side, are of the readily available stone.

Hereford, Hereford & Worcester ☆   MAP A

At Broomy Hill, one mile west of the city centre, is the Herefordshire
Waterworks Museum, where the processes involved in a public water
supply in Victorian times can be seen. Several large pumping engines of the
period are preserved. Open some afternoons in the summer months. Tel:
Hereford 2487.

High Wycombe, Buckinghamshire □   MAP A

The furniture factories and timber yards in and around High Wycombe are
the modern industrial outcome of a former woodland craft of the Chiltern

beechwoods, when independent workers commonly known as 'chair-bodgers' made chair-legs, stools, tent pegs and spokes for wagon wheels, among other things. The men and the woods were interdependent, the 'bodgers' selectively felling only such trees as would encourage the straight and upright growth of saplings by providing sufficient light and space, so that new timber was always replacing that taken away. The only machine used by these craftsmen was a pole-lathe, the earliest device invented for turning wood. A hemp rope was attached to one end of a long pole, usually of larch, and wound round the wood to be turned. The other end of the pole was attached to a treadle, which exploited the natural springiness of the pole, tightening the rope to turn the wood one way, then relying on the spring in the pole to turn it the other way as the rope was released. With this gadget a skilled man could make eight hundred chair legs a week, which he delivered to factories in London and other centres where the complete chairs were assembled, until the rise of High Wycombe itself as the centre of furniture making, early in the nineteenth century. The town's factories now produce more than three quarters of all the wooden chairs made in Britain. The town's museum in Queen Victoria Street has a pole-lathe and examples of local products, including the 'Windsor' chair, first made here.

Hinckley, Leicestershire □   MAP A

In Lower Bond Street is a row of thatched framework-knitters' cottages, of timber-framed construction with brick infilling. The rows of upper floor windows at the back can be seen from the car park behind them. The first stocking frame in the county was set up at Hinckley in 1640 by William Iliffe, and the town has prospered on hosiery manufacturing ever since. One of the town's biggest modern factories makes a startling contrast on the opposite side of the road. The hosiery industry is remarkable for the fact that the early framework knitters were men assisted by their womenfolk as seamers and by their children in the hard times of the Luddite troubles. But by the 1930s, the factory industry employed mainly women and girls, who could produce three hundred million pairs of stockings a year in Leicestershire alone.

Holkham, Norfolk ▲   MAP A

Holkham Hall was the home of the famous agricultural pioneer Thomas Coke, universally known as Coke of Norfolk, who became Earl of Leicester five years before his death in 1842. On the estate is Longlands Farm, at the southern end of the park, a model farm with its own sawmill, foundry and forge; and there is a museum collection of bygones which include traction engines and agricultural equipment. Open certain weekdays in summer. Tel: Fakenham 710227.

Holme Fen, Cambridgeshire ▲   MAP A

The original Holme Fen Post at this nature reserve near Peterborough was a cast-iron pillar from the Great Exhibition, driven 22 feet into the peat in 1851 to prove the theory that the Fens were sinking as the water was drained away from them in land reclamation. Within half a century, 12 feet of the post was exposed, and in 1957 a new post was sunk to reveal the continuing story of the sinking surface level, which is now about 14 feet lower than it was in 1848.

Honiton, Devon +   MAP A

Devon has a greater mileage of roads than any other English county, and all holiday-makers travelling to the resorts of Devon and Cornwall, before the building of the Honiton by-pass, knew the town as a frightful bottleneck. The road through it to Exeter was always a busy and important highway, and the Honiton Turnpike Trust, set up in 1753, was one of the first in Devon. Toll-booths were established on all the entrance roads to the town. The only surviving toll-house is the so-called Copper Castle, outside the town on the Axminster road (A35). It is a single-storey castellated building with Gothic windows in its rounded front and each side of its little porch, giving the keeper a view of the road in both directions. He collected his coppers from all passing vehicles before opening the wrought-iron toll gates, which are still there, though now, of course, disused.

Horkstow, Humberside +   MAP B

At this village near Barton-upon-Humber, where the new Humber Bridge commences its crossing of the estuary, a rather more modest suspension bridge survives from 1844. It is one of the works of Sir John Rennie, built to cross the New River Ancholme, and has a span of 130 feet. Rusticated masonry arches stand at each end of the bridge, which is now used only for farm access.

Huddersfield, West Yorkshire =   MAP B

Huddersfield's railway station, built in 1847–8, is one of the most impressive early station buildings in the country. It was designed for the London and North Western Railway by J.P. Pritchett and consists of a central block with Corinthian portico, flanked by colonnaded wings.

Huddersfield, West Yorkshire ☆ MAP B

The Tolson Memorial Museum is in Ravensknowle Park, where some parts of the town's eighteenth-century Cloth Hall have been re-erected, after the historic building's demolition in 1930 to make way for a cinema – the local product was displaced by fantasies woven in Hollywood. The museum is mainly concerned with the local textile industry, and is particularly good on the period of the Luddite riots. There is also a banner carried during a demonstration in York against child slavery, organized by Richard Oastler (*q.v.*) in 1832. The museum is open throughout the year. Tel: Huddersfield 30591.

Hull, Humberside ○ MAP B

At the end of the seventeenth century Defoe reckoned that Hull did more trade than any other town of its size in Europe, with the local merchants shipping goods from all over northern and eastern England to the Continent, and importing goods from the European ports. Early in the nineteenth century, John Rennie built the Humber Dock, to be followed later by Prince's Dock (1829), Railway Dock (1846) and Victoria Dock (1850), with their bridges, locks and warehouses. By this time the port was the third largest in England for imports, after London and Liverpool, and was only beaten into fourth place for exports by Newcastle. Its wharves were among the few where steam vessels outnumbered sailing ships at that time. Much damage was done to Hull by bombing in the Second World War, and the site of its first dock, built in the eighteenth century, is now a garden.

Hull, Humberside ▲ MAP B

In Queen Victoria Square is the Town Docks Museum, exhibiting the history of shipping and the fisheries of Hull, and in particular the Greenland whaling industry. Hull has one of the country's largest trawler fleets. The museum is open every day from May to September except Sunday mornings. Tel: Hull 223111.

Hutton-le-Hole, North Yorkshire ☆   MAP B

Despite Hutton-le-Hole's well-deserved reputation as one of the most
picturesque villages of North Yorkshire, its origins are industrial, since it
was built largely by the Quaker owners of local iron mines in the eighteenth
century. There is no 'steeple house' (church) in the village, and the inn is
called the 'Hammer and Hand', from the inscription 'By Hammer and
Hand all Arts do stand' (a highly debatable proposition). The chief
industrial interest in the village now, however, is the Ryedale Folk
Museum, accommodated in some converted farm buildings. Various local
crafts and agricultural implements are represented, but there is also a
blacksmith's forge and a Tudor glass furnace, discovered in Rosedale (*q.v.*)
in 1968, and carefully dismantled and re-erected here in an ambitious
piece of preservation work like a sort of Abu Simbel operation in miniature.
The museum is open daily during the summer months. Tel: Kirkbymoor-
side 367.

Hythe, Kent ≈   MAP A

The Royal Military Canal was completed in 1806, running from the sea
near Hythe to Winchelsea in East Sussex, and was designed as a 30-mile-
long defensive ditch against anticipated Napoleonic invasion. It cut Romney Marsh off from the mainland. William Cobbett poured scorn on 'Pitt's
ditch', asking if a 30-foot-wide canal was to keep at bay an army which had
crossed the Rhine and the Danube. There was more to this canal than just a
final obstacle, however. Its sluices could be used to flood the whole area if it
became infested with invading forces. Fortunately, its effectiveness was
never put to the test. Nowadays, the canal serves as a vital part of Romney
Marsh's drainage system, and provides leisure facilities for boating and
fishing. At Hythe, it runs through the town and is lined with trees.

Ilfracombe, Devon ×   MAP A

At Hele, a mile east of the town centre, there is a sixteenth-century corn
mill powered by an overshot waterwheel of 18-foot diameter. The mill has
been restored and can be seen grinding wholemeal flour on weekdays and
Sunday afternoons between Easter and October.

Inverness, Highland ☐   MAP D

Parts of Pringles' famous Holm Mills date from around 1780, when the small original mill was powered by waterwheel. Overwhelming competition from Yorkshire to Scotland's traditional woollen industry during the Industrial Revolution forced Scottish manufacturers to specialize in high-quality fashion knitwear, and visitors here can see the processes involved in making the firm's lambswool garments. Open on working days most of the year. Tel: Inverness 223311.

Iona, Strathclyde △ MAP D

The tiny island associated with the spread of Christianity to Britain has also been exploited for its stone – the only true marble quarried in Britain. It is white with yellowy-green streaks and mottling, and can be seen in the island's cathedral. The quarries, on the island's south-east side, are now derelict.

Ironbridge, Shropshire + MAP B

The Iron Bridge spanning the River Severn is perhaps the world's best-known industrial monument. It was commenced by Abraham Darby II and completed by his son in 1780, the world's first bridge built of iron. A Shrewsbury architect, Thomas Farnolls Pritchard, had the idea and drew up the original plan, but the design was modified in the process of building the bridge. The hundred-foot single-span bridge is supported by masonry abutments on both banks of the river. Its chief original purpose was to facilitate transportation by road of the products of the Coalbrookdale iron works (q.v.), which had previously been conveyed by river and canal transport. Coalbrookdale acted like a magnet on artists, most of whom painted romantic images of the iron bridge in its wooded valley setting, and the bridge itself was soon being promoted as a tourist attraction. It is still an impressive sight from the river banks after two centuries, but is unequal to modern road traffic and is now accessible only to pedestrians.

Ironbridge Gorge, Shropshire ☆ MAP B

The Ironbridge Gorge Museum is an extensive open-air museum embracing the buildings and industrial remains of the former cradle of the Industrial Revolution, centred on Coalbrookdale (q.v.), now part of the new town named after the great civil engineer Thomas Telford (q.v.) who was once Shropshire's Surveyor of Public Works. The museum preserves, among many other industrial monuments, the famous Iron Bridge (q.v.); the Old Furnace at Coalbrookdale in which Darby (q.v.) successfully used

coke for smelting; the Hay Incline which was built in 1793 to raise tub boats 207 feet from one canal level to another; a pair of double-beam blast-furnace blowing engines known as David and Sampson (*sic*); the former Great Warehouse of the Coalbrookdale Company; the china works at Coalport (*q.v.*); the so-called Bedlam Furnaces built especially for coke smelting in 1757–8; and the pithead winding gear of Blists Hill mine. The museum is open daily throughout the year. Tel: Ironbridge 3522.

 Kelso, Borders +   MAP D

The fine stone road bridge across the Tweed was built in 1803 by John Rennie, the great engineer and bridge-builder who modelled London's old Waterloo Bridge on this, his first major bridge. It has 5 elliptical arches of 72-foot span.

Kelston, Avon □   MAP A

Brass-founding became an important industry of this region in the eight-

eenth century, and by mid-century the Avon valley between Bristol and
Bath was the chief centre of British brass-founding and manufacture. The
reason was largely geographical. Brass is an alloy of copper and zinc; the
one metal was imported at Bristol docks (*q.v.*) from the mines in Cornwall,
and the other mined in the Mendip Hills nearby. One of the first brass mills
in the region was set up by Abraham Darby (*q.v.*) in 1702, but by 1930 the
industry was extinct in the area, having been taken over by Birmingham. At
Kelston, north-west of the village centre, the buildings of a former brass
mill remain, with the distinctive stone tapering chimneys of annealing
furnaces beside the River Avon. They were in use until the middle of the
nineteenth century, and are now part of a marina complex. Annealing was
the heating and slow cooling process by which the resulting metal was
toughened.

Kendal, Cumbria ☆ MAP B

The Museum of Lakeland Life and Industry at Abbot Hall was the first
winner (in 1973) of the Museum of the Year Award. There are exhibits on
many local industries, including bobbin-making, mining and quarrying, as
well as examples of Neolithic tools and implements made in the region.
The museum is open every day except winter bank holidays – afternoons
only during weekends. Tel: Kendal 22464.

Kendal, Cumbria ☐ MAP B

One of the more unlikely specialities of Lake District industry was
snuff-making – a by-product of the huge tobacco trade with America. The
business grew from about the middle of the eighteenth century and became
concentrated in and around Kendal, with seven mills grinding snuff (which
is powdered tobacco) at one time. A mile and a half to the south of the town,
on the west bank of the River Kent at Helsington, are two rubble-stone
mills with workers' cottages. One of the mills still produces snuff. The
other still has *in situ* the wooden undershot waterwheel installed to drive its
grinding machinery.

Kidsgrove, Staffordshire ≈ MAP B

West of the parish church are the entrances to the two Harecastle Tunnels
on the Trent and Mersey Canal. The first tunnel was designed by James
Brindley (*q.v.*) and took 11 years to complete, from 1766 to 1777. Brindley
died before it was finished. It was 2,880 yards in length and 9 feet 3 inches

wide. In 1824, Telford (*q.v.*) began a new tunnel, both longer and wider. It was 2,926 yards long and 14 feet wide, but it took only 3 years to complete because of more advanced engineering methods. The reasons for the new tunnel were that the old one was a terrible bottleneck, and that it was unsafe. It was so narrow that barges had worn the brickwork to half its normal thickness in scraping through, and mining subsidence was also causing it to crumble. There had been complaints for many years from the canal's users, fed up with waiting in long queues at one end for the procession of boats to clear from the other; like sitting at traffic lights that never change to green. The surveyors for the new tunnel reckoned that no tunnel except Brindley's before it had ever been driven through such hard rock. Telford sank fifteen working shafts from Harecastle Hill down to the tunnel and speeded up the work by operating in several parts at once. Boulton and Watt beam engines pumped out water at both ends, and a brick yard was set up to make the bricks near the site – seven million were used. The tunnel was one of the greatest engineering feats in the history of the canals, and, as Telford proudly reported, not a single life was lost.

Kielder, Northumberland   =   MAP B

The skew-arch railway viaduct was built in 1862 to carry a branch line of the Border Counties Railway across the valley of the Kielder Burn. Built of stone with battlemented parapets, it involved intricate geometrical shaping of the masonry, and though the line was closed thirty years ago, the bridge has been preserved as an example of Victorian railway engineering.

King's Lynn, Norfolk   o   MAP A

King's Lynn was one of the busiest seaports in the country in the Middle Ages, and although the sea has receded, leaving the town inland, it is still a busy place on the Great Ouse. In the nineteenth century two docks were built, the Alexandra and the Bentinck, capable of handling large ships from the Continent. Visitors cannot enter the docks without a permit, but Cross Bank Road passes between them and offers a glimpse of their warehouse buildings and activity. A little way up-river near the town centre is the fine Customs House, built in 1683.

King's Mills, Leicestershire   □   MAP A

This interesting industrial complex beside the River Trent near Castle

Donington is a well known local beauty spot. The earliest mill here was recorded in Domesday Book, and later there were as many as five, occupied in grinding corn, malting, fulling and paper-making. There is a suggestion that banknote paper was made here once, and there is also evidence of a button factory where a row of cottages now stands. One of the waterwheels that drove machinery here was said to be the biggest in England. Three rusted iron wheels remain at the site, but otherwise all that can be seen are foundations and watercourses. The road to the site passes beneath an unusual chain bridge crossing between the high banks to give access for residents.

Kirkcudbright, Dumfries & Galloway   +   MAP D

The Tongueland Bridge crossing the River Dee (A755) was the first bridge built in Scotland by Telford (q.v.). It is a masonry bridge with a single arch of 112 feet span, and was completed in 1806. It was unusual in two respects. Telford gave it hollow spandrels to lighten the load on the foundations, which also gives a deceptive appearance of lightness to the structure; and the roadway does not rise to the crown of the arch, which was usually done to ensure that rainwater would not lie on the road surface.

 ## Lacock, Wiltshire ▲   MAP A

On the A350 north of the village is the museum of the Lackham College of Agriculture, open to the public on certain days each year or by prior arrangement. There are exhibits on all aspects of agriculture, and the museum has an interesting collection of farming implements and machines, including old tractors. Tel: Chippenham 3251.

Lake Vyrnwy, Powys   ☆   MAP C

The damming of the River Vyrnwy in 1881–92 to create a reservoir to supply Liverpool with water involved the earliest large-scale masonry dam, 161 feet high and 390 yards long. A turreted tower on the lakeside behind the dam contains the supply controls at the point where the aqueduct begins its 75-mile journey to Liverpool. Tablets near the northern end of the dam, which carries a roadway, record details of its construction.

Lambley, Northumberland   =   MAP B

The masonry railway viaduct was built for the Newcastle and Carlisle

Railway in 1852, and crosses the South Tyne at a height of 110 feet above the river. It has 9 arches with above-average spans of 58 feet.

Lanark, Strathclyde + MAP D

The most dramatic of the bridges built in Scotland by Thomas Telford (*q.v.*) is undoubtedly the Cartland Crags Bridge, which crosses the gorge of Mouse Water just north west of Lanark. Completed in 1822, it carries the road 129 feet above the stream by means of three stone arches.

Lancaster, Lancashire + MAP B

The Skerton Bridge carrying the A6 over the River Lune was built in 1788 to the design of Thomas Harrison of Chester, at a cost of £14,000. It is said to have been the first large bridge in the country made with a level roadway (i.e. not rising towards the crown). It is a masonry bridge of five elliptical arches with a stone balustrade.

Opposite
*The Great
Wheel of Laxey*

Lancaster, Lancashire   ○   MAP B

The tidal estuary of the River Lune gave rise to Lancaster's development as an inland port in the eighteenth century, trading with the West Indies, and several contemporary warehouses survive along St George's Quay as well as the fine Custom House, designed in Palladian style by Richard Gillow and built in 1764. The warehouses are built of stone and have wooden beam hoists on the gable walls. Later, new ports were developed at Sunderland Point and Glasson for larger ships than could negotiate the estuary as far as Lancaster itself.

Lancaster, Lancashire   ≈   MAP B

North-east of the town is the Lune Aqueduct, built in 1797 to carry the Lancaster Canal over the river. It is 640 feet long and is supported on 5 masonry arches. It is an elegant structure of the local grey sandstone, with a balustrade and cornice, and was one of the works of the canal's engineer John Rennie, one of the great exponents of stone bridges, though much of the credit for this one must go to the architect, Alexander Stevens.

Laxey, Isle of Man   ×   MAP B

There are *older* waterwheels than the famous 'Lady Isabella' here, but none greater. The massive 72-foot wheel of iron and wood was built by Robert Casement in 1854 to pump water from a deep lead mine. The idea of increasing the diameter in waterwheels was that the number of 'buckets' could be increased and so the bigger the wheel the more power was generated. The Laxey wheel had 168 buckets, each holding 24 gallons. The operation of the wheel is unusual, being a variation on the overshot type in which water falls on to the top of the wheel and turns it in the same direction as the water's flow. Here the wheel is of 'pitchback' type, the water falling short of the highest point of the wheel, and thus turning it, as it were, backwards, or in the opposite direction to the flow of water. A reservoir had to be constructed to drive the wheel, which is some distance away from the pump shaft. Lady Isabella was the wife of the island's governor. The wheel was in commercial use until 1926, and since the 1960s has been in operation as a tourist attraction, maintained by the Manx Government.

Laxton, Nottinghamshire ▲   MAP B

This site will rarely be found in books on 'industrial archaeology', which usually show scant interest in agriculture. But in any reference to useful labour it occupies a significant place as a village where the medieval open field system of farming has survived in some degree. Around the church, cottages and the remains of the county's largest motte-and-bailey castle are the three large fields, only parts of which have ever been enclosed, where the feudal system of agriculture was practised a thousand years ago. They are still much the same in appearance as they were then, and farmed in much the same way, although tractors have now replaced teams of oxen. One field is left fallow each year and the other two divided into strips which are shared out among the farmers. The fields are still known as South Field, West Field and Mill Field, and are registered as an Ancient Monument.

Leadhills, Strathclyde △   MAP D

The name tells all. Lead was mined at several sites in Scotland's Lowther Hills, and there are interesting remains of the industry here, which operated for about six centuries. It is widely believed that the mines also produced gold which was used in the crowns of Scotland's kings. At Wanlockhead, to the south, the Straitsteps mine remains include a primitive water-powered beam engine for draining the mine. The engine is scheduled as an Ancient Monument, though it may not be older than the late nineteenth century.

Leeds, West Yorkshire ☐   MAP B

In Marshall Street are the Temple Works, built in 1840, one of the more surprising eccentricities of Yorkshire's hard-headed textile manufacturers. Ignatious Bonomi and David Roberts designed and built for John Marshall a mill for the preparation and spinning of flax. Taking a hint from the fame and antiquity of Egyptian flax working, Roberts went off to the banks of the Nile to study the Temple of Karnak, and came back to build Mr Marshall a factory in like fashion, which soon became known, naturally enough, as the Temple Mill. Columns of cast iron doubled as drainpipes and supports for the ceiling, which had domed skylights. The front of the building has six recessed Egyptian lotus columns flanking the windows and supporting a long entablature. Even the original factory chimney was designed as an Egyptian obelisk, though this subsequently cracked and had to be replaced by something rather more conventionally Victorian. Marshall's flax business declined after his death and closed down altogether in 1886, but the building remains standing (and occupied) as a monument to the slight attack of megalomania that Yorkshire's textile industry went through in the nineteenth century.

Leeds, West Yorkshire □   MAP B

In Thwaite Lane, at Hunslet, is the Thwaite Putty Mill, one of the last places in England to keep waterwheels in regular use. Until recent years, two iron breastshot wheels driven by the River Aire ran machinery here which ground chalk for making putty. The largest wheel has a diameter of 17 feet 10 inches and is over 14 feet wide. It was built in 1825, originally for crushing flint used in glazing pottery. The complex includes offices, stables and other ancillary buildings of red brick. One of the curiosities of water mills is that in the North, unlike the South of England, the wheels are usually erected *inside* the buildings.

Leek, Staffordshire ✕   MAP B

Leek is a town of many textile mills, but Brindley's Mill, on the A523 Macclesfield road, is especially interesting as a survival of the early work of James Brindley (*q.v.*). It is a two-storey mill (now open to the public) which he built in 1752, though it has been much altered since that time. Open weekend and bank holiday afternoons, Easter to October.

Leicester, Leicestershire ☆   MAP A

The Abbey Lane Pumping Station at the junction of the Leicester Canal with the River Soar, a mile north of the city centre in Corporation Road, was built in 1891 as a sewage pumping works. It was built with the characteristic ostentation of the period, and looks like a Victorian town hall with a chimney. Its brick engine house is now the centrepiece of an industrial museum, containing four large beam engines built by the local firm Gimsons, who opened their Vulcan Works in 1842 to build light machinery for Leicester's important footwear industry. The museum is open every day except Fridays and Sunday mornings throughout the year. Tel: Leicester 661330.

Glassworks a:
Lemington

Lemington, Tyne & Wear □   MAP B

The glass cone at Lemington, although incomplete, is one of few such survivals in Britain, and particularly in the region where the Venerable Bede tells us that French glassmakers were brought over to teach the 'English nation their handicraft', which had been lost here after the departure of the Romans. Because of the national shortage of timber in the Stuart period, James I banned the use of wood to fuel glass furnaces, and the need for coal supplies contributed to the rise in importance of glass making in Scotland and the North of England. The Lemington cone was built in 1787 and was 130 feet high. It was originally one of four at the site, belonging to the Northumberland Glass Company.

Lemsford, Hertfordshire ×   MAP A

The four-storey flour mill built of brick and weatherboarding on the River Lea dates from the early nineteenth century, and cast-iron columns were used, relatively early, for the interior structure. The machinery was driven by an overshot waterwheel. The mill is said to have inspired J.P. Skelly's famous song, 'There's an old mill by the stream, Nelly Dean,' but the waters hardly murmur soft and low nowadays, for their sound is drowned by the roar of traffic on the nearby A1(M).

Lerwick, Shetland   ○   MAP D

Houses on the harbour of the Shetlands' capital have 'lodberries'. These are piers built out over the harbour, and indicate old merchants' houses, where ships could unload directly into the premises. Shipping and seafaring are among the exhibits in the town's Shetland County Museum.

Letterston, Dyfed   □   MAP C

At this village off the A40 south of Fishguard is the Tregwynt Woollen Mill, which dates from the middle of the eighteenth century and has been in continuous production of woollen yarns since then. It is particularly noted for blankets. Its early machinery was driven by waterwheel. Visitors can see the mill in operation at any time during normal working hours.

Limpley Stoke, Wiltshire   ≈   MAP A

Three miles south-east of Bath, off the A36, is the Dundas Aqueduct, which carries the Kennet and Avon Canal over the Avon. It was designed by the canal's engineer, John Rennie, built in 1800, and is a fine 3-arched masonry structure of local Bath limestone, with a main span of 64½ feet flanked by Doric pilasters.

Lincoln, Lincolnshire   ≈   MAP B

Brayford Pool, locally known as the 'Glory Hole', is a basin south-west of the city centre where the River Witham meets the Foss Dyke (*see* Torksey). The river passes beneath High Bridge, a remarkable twelfth-century stone bridge which has half-timbered shops on it – the oldest bridge in Britain still to support buildings. The basin is linked to three thousand miles of inland waterways, and so had a busy commercial life at one time, and a few of its old warehouses remain.

Littleborough, Greater Manchester   □   MAP B

Littleborough is interesting as a weaving town which saw the beginning of the rise of cotton mills, but fell behind when the great boom concentrated the industry in the palatial brick mills of Manchester, Oldham, Rochdale, Bolton, *et al.* Here the building material is stone, and there are weavers' cottages with their long mullioned windows on the upper floors, as well as early water-powered mills, of which the two-storey Clough Mill is characteristic. Such early mills were closely packed with looms, operated by both men and women, who would run three or four looms each.

Little Longstone, Derbyshire   =   MAP B

The Monsal Dale Viaduct was built in 1862 to carry the Midland Railway across the valley of the River Wye, so that, as Ruskin put it, 'every fool in Buxton can be in Bakewell in half an hour'. The massive stone structure has acquired a mature and acceptable appearance in these days of so much brick and concrete, and it is one of the ironies of the philosophy of conservation that the blessed bridge which Ruskin regarded as a monstrous intrusion into a beautiful natural scene should, a hundred years later, have been noisily protected from demolition by the very people who would presumably have sided with Ruskin in wishing to preserve the landscape.

Liverpool, Merseyside   ○   MAP B

Liverpool's dockland is much too complex to be described in detail in a work of this kind, and is in any case largely inaccessible to the general public, but Albert Dock, which you can visit, is of particular interest and importance. Liverpool was a relative late-comer to the great docks of Britain, having risen to prominence in the eighteenth century through the cotton trade, importing raw cotton and (like Bristol [*q.v.*]) having a lively traffic in slaves, as well as exporting cotton goods. The chief architect of the subsequent dock system built in the nineteenth century was Jesse Hartley, and Albert Dock is his greatest monument. It was modelled loosely on London's St Katharine Dock (*q.v.*) and covers seven acres. The dock was built during 1841–5 with five-storey fireproof warehouses of granite, brick and cast iron on all sides. Massive cast-iron pillars form Doric colonnades along the ground-floor frontages. At the dock's entrance is a cast-iron swing bridge. In the years when Hartley was building Albert Dock and other extensions of the system, Liverpool was rapidly becoming established as the second most important port in Britain, and Albert Dock, which has outlived its usefulness, stands as a monument both to Hartley and to Liverpool's Victorian prosperity.

Liverpool, Merseyside ☆   MAP B

Oriel Chambers, at the corner of Water Street and Covent Garden, is, according to Sir Nikolaus Pevsner, 'one of the most remarkable buildings of its date in Europe'. It was built in 1864 to the design of a local architect, Peter Ellis, and is of five storeys. Its street frontages are mostly of glass, separated by stone mullions designed to look like cast iron, and the windows are constructed as oriels in very slender iron frames; it is included in this book because it was a pioneering metal-framed building.

Llanberis, Gwynedd =   MAP C

The town is the terminus of the unique narrow-gauge (2 feet 7½ inches) rack-and-pinion Snowdon Mountain Railway, which has the steepest gradient (1 in 52) of any locomotive track in Britain, and climbs to a height of just under 3,500 feet. The line was opened in 1896, but the engine jumped the rails on its maiden run, and modifications had to be made before the service could be resumed. Swiss-inclined boiler locomotives are used on the line, and the train takes one hour to travel the 4½ miles to the summit. The railway runs from April to October.

Llanfair P.G., Anglesey +   MAP C

On the Holyhead road at Llanfairpwllgwyngyllgogerychwyrndrobwllllantysiliogogogoch, now mercifully abbreviated to Llanfair P.G., is a white toll-house on the former turnpike road, part of the new Holyhead route engineered by Telford (q.v.). The toll-board here is, unusually, still intact, showing dues charged for various types of vehicle, including double the standard toll for a wagon whose tyres were fastened with projecting instead of countersunk nails.

Loan End, Northumberland +   MAP B

The almost fragile-looking Union Chain Bridge crossing the River Tweed to link England and Scotland is the earliest surviving suspension bridge in the country, though contemporary with work on Telford's Menai Bridge (q.v.). It was designed by Sir Samuel Brown (then Captain Brown of the Royal Navy) and built in 1820. The chains supporting the deck of timber

Opposite
*Water pump
at Kew Steam
Museum*
are made of wrought-iron links which Brown had patented three years
earlier. The masonry suspension tower on the English bank is of different
design from that on the Scottish side. Strengthening and repair operations
have been carried out on the bridge from time to time, including the
addition of steel cables to assist the original chains.

London – Brentford   ✕   MAP A

Between the River Thames and the M4 viaduct to the west of Kew Bridge
are the Kew Bridge Waterworks, where the best collection of *in situ*
pumping engines in the world is now preserved by a trust as the Kew Bridge
Living Steam Museum. Nineteenth-century Boulton and Watt, Maudsley
and Harvey beam engines are here, where until the end of the Second
World War they supplied water to west London. The museum is open at
weekends. Tel: 01-568-4757.

London – Camden   =   MAP A

What was until recently the Round House Arts Centre in Chalk Farm Road
was originally built as a locomotive turntable shed for the London and
North Western Railway. It was designed by George Stephenson (*q.v.*) and
built in 1847. Cast-iron columns and a curved rib framework support the
conical roof which has a diameter of 180 feet.

London – Hampstead   +   MAP A

At the north end of Spaniards Road, crossing Hampstead Heath, is a
restored eighteenth-century toll-house, opposite the Spaniards Inn. It is a
single-storey building of brick. Turnpike roads existed for over two
hundred years, being finally abolished in 1895. They were introduced in
the seventeenth century as a method of paying for the upkeep of highways
when other methods had failed. The appalling condition of the highways
out of London and in the northern Home Counties is attested to by many
travellers of the time, especially Defoe. A gate closed the road until the
toll-house keeper had collected the due amount from each vehicle passing
in either direction. Later toll-houses were usually built with a projecting
bay having windows flanking the door at roughly 45° angles so that the
keeper could see approaching traffic in both directions.

London – Holborn   +   MAP A

The viaduct built by William Haywood in 1869, carrying the road between the City and the West End over Farringdon Street, is ¼ mile in length and is supported by a cast-iron span of 107 feet between its piers. The line of Farringdon Street was originally the valley of the Fleet River, known at its upper part here as 'Hole Bourne'. The river is now carried below Farringdon Street by a sewer. Holborn Viaduct is decorated with assorted figures and the arms of the City, and is best seen from Farringdon Street.

London – Kensington   ☆   MAP A

The Science Museum in Exhibition Road is a must for those interested in the mechanics, as opposed to the sociology, of our industrial development. It is packed with exhibits on the application of science to industry and technology, and there are many working models of machinery and equipment as well as full-size machines, engines and instruments. The museum's collection is vast, for it covers everything from windmills to space exploration. It is open throughout the year. Tel: 01-589-3456.

London – Kew   ☐   MAP A

The Palm House in the Royal Botanic Gardens was built 1844–8, and is one of the most startling pieces of Victorian architectural audacity, qualifying for a place in this book by virtue of its function and its pioneering construction. Designed and built by Richard Turner and Decimus Burton, this gigantic conservatory of glass in a delicate framework of iron is 362 feet long and 62 feet high at its centre. All its roofs are curved. It preceded the building of the Crystal Palace for the Great Exhibition of 1851, and served as an inspiration, if not a model, for it, but is actually superior to it in design.

London – Paddington   =   MAP A

The train shed of Paddington Station was the terminus of the Great Western Railway, and was built by Brunel (*q.v.*) and Matthew Digby-Wyatt in 1854. Columns of cast iron support roofs of wrought iron and glass over the three original bays (the fourth is a more recent addition), and an oriel above Platform 1 was the Station Master's vantage point.

London – Rotherhithe   =   MAP A

The Metropolitan line between Wapping and Rotherhithe on the underground system passes through the Thames Tunnel, the first tunnel built
beneath the river. It was begun in 1825 by the Brunels, father and son (*q.v.*),
but was not completed until 1843 due to various delaying factors which
included disastrous floods. The tunnel is 1,200 yards long, and at the
Rotherhithe side, in Tunnel Road, is the engine house built for steam-
driven pumps during construction. The tunnel was a failure both financial-
ly and in terms of use, being intended for pedestrians, and in 1865 it was
converted for use by the London Underground. The road on which
Rotherhithe Station stands is called Brunel Road.

London – St Katharine Dock   ○   MAP A

Immediately to the east of the Tower of London and Tower Bridge are
these docks, which were constructed during 1825–8 and are the farthest
upstream of the Thames docks. Their purpose was to provide unloading
and warehousing facilities as close to the heart of London as possible, and
Thomas Telford (*q.v.*) and Philip Hardwick were appointed chief engineer
and architect respectively. The six-storey warehouses were designed by
Telford to stand by the water's edge so that goods could be moved by crane
straight from ship to warehouse without the double handling usual in docks
of the time. During the Second World War considerable damage was done
to the docks by enemy action, and they have now been restored as part of
the World Trade Centre, with the dock as a yachting harbour and the
surviving warehouses used as trading floors with shops beneath, an
imaginative example of redevelopment combined with conservation.

London – St Pancras   =   MAP A

The Gothic facade of St Pancras Station was the work of Sir George
Gilbert Scott, and was built between 1867 and 1874. The station was a
terminus of the Midland Railway, and W.H. Barlow designed the single-
span iron and glass roof of the train shed, which has a length of 690 feet and
a then unprecedented span of 243 feet. Scott's building was formerly the
Midland Grand Hotel, and is built of brick with stone dressings. It is one of
the monuments of Victorian architecture in London, and has a 300-foot
clock tower among its varied features influenced by French and Italian
models.

London's Dockland   ○

From East Ham and Woolwich, upstream through Greenwich, Deptford and Rotherhithe, Isle of Dogs, Limehouse, Wapping and Stepney, the great system of commercial docks begun in the Middle Ages stretches along the Thames where, as long ago as the Roman occupation, the estuary's great potential was realized. The Romans built the first quays on the river whose mouth is opposite those of the Rhine and the Maas; from these quays ships could penetrate deep into Europe. Chaucer worked in the first Customs House, and Pepys saw the building of the first wet dock at Blackwall. By Stuart times, over eighty per cent of Britain's imports were passing through London. The East India Company expanded the docks at Blackwall, whaling ships operated from the Greenland Dock at Bermondsey, and tea clippers were familiar vessels on the river. Early in the nineteenth century, development of the London and West India docks was made, with massive warehouse systems, to handle the largest ships then afloat. The nineteenth century also brought a huge expansion of the dock system downstream with the Royal Docks entered from the stretch of the river known as Galleons Reach. The Royal Victoria, Royal Albert and King George V docks comprise the largest impounded docks in the world. Meanwhile, Bristol, Liverpool and Glasgow (*qq.v.*) had grown to give London plenty of competition, and in the last forty years Rotterdam has overtaken London in the annual tonnage it handles. But the development of Tilbury, twenty miles downstream, to cope with huge supertankers and modern container handling has kept London in the forefront of commercial shipping. Some of the old docks have been closed now, and there is no public admission to those still working, but the special atmosphere of the dockland industry can be savoured in the streets around them. The National Maritime Museum at Greenwich presents a survey of maritime history from the Tudor period up to the present day. At Greenwich Pier, the last surviving sailing clipper, *Cutty Sark*, is moored permanently and can be visited.

London – Spitalfields   ☆

In and around Fournier Street, east of Spitalfields Market, are several eighteenth-century houses once occupied by the weavers who made the district famous for its woven silk. Huguenot refugees from France settled here in what became one of London's ghettoes in the eighteenth century, and brought their weaving skills with them. (In Artillery Lane, nearby, there is a warehouse which was originally a Huguenot chapel.) The area had been built up where not long before, according to Defoe's account, there were fields of grass with cows feeding in them. The weavers' houses are easily recognizable by the obvious addition of the attic floors, with their continuous rows of windows for maximum light, to the original three-storey brick terraces. From its beginnings here, silk weaving spread to the Midlands and the north where it graduated to factory industry status.

London – Strand ☆   MAP A

In Carting Lane, off the south side of the Strand beside the Savoy Hotel, is an ornate iron gas lamp dating from the end of the nineteenth century, and a survival of J.E. Webb's Patent Sewer Lamps, which extracted gas from the sewers below the streets and burned it for street lighting.

London – Tower Bridge +   MAP A

England's best known bridge was built across the Thames in 1888–94, and cost over a million pounds. It is the farthest bridge downstream on the river. The bridge was originally designed by Sir Horace Jones, the City Architect, who died as the work was commenced, and John Wolfe Barry then
Tower Bridge   modified the drawbridge design, assisted by Brunel (*q.v.*). The twin

drawbridges, or 'bascules', forming the central section of the roadway, weigh about a thousand tons each, and can be raised in a minute and a half to allow large vessels to pass through. This was originally done by steam engines with hydraulic pumps. Since 1977 the bridge has been electrically operated, but one of the steam engines is preserved *in situ*. The engine room is beneath the south approach to the bridge. The two Gothic towers are of steel cased in granite and Portland (*q.v.*) stone, and a footbridge (permanently closed) runs between them, 140 feet above water level.

London – Wallington +   MAP A

The grounds of the public library at Wallington seem an unlikely setting for industrial remains, but here can be seen a preserved section of tramway used by the Surrey Iron Railway, the first tramway built as a transport system independent of canal and other industrial transport. It was opened in 1803, and was a horse-drawn tramway built by William Jessop to cover the nine miles between Wandsworth and Croydon. It was intended at one stage to extend the line as far as Portsmouth!

London – Westminster ☆   MAP A

A plaque on a wall is admittedly not much to look at for those with a passion for working machinery and dramatic industrial landscapes, but this one marks the site of the foundation of that industry which has had a greater impact on civilization than any other. On the wall of the south transept aisle of Westminster Abbey is a tablet recording the setting up by William Caxton in 1477 of Britain's first printing press. Caxton had learned the art of printing from movable types in Cologne, and set up his press in the abbey precincts, close to the chapter house, where he printed books under the patronage of the English kings Edward IV, Richard III and Henry VII. Caxton's successor after his death was Wynkyn de Worde, whose own press was 'at the signe of the Swane' in Fleet Street, the chief centre of printed information in Britain ever since. The vast and highly mechanized modern industry of printing, which can be found in every town and city in the kingdom, has been dispersed during five hundred years from this one spot which ought to be holy ground to the industrialist as well as the Christian.

Longdon-upon-Tern, Shropshire ≈   MAP B

In a field alongside the main road through the village is the first complete cast-iron aqueduct ever built. It was constructed by Telford (*q.v.*) in 1796 to carry the Shrewsbury Canal over the River Tern, and was very much a piece of engineering experiment at the time, to be carried to glorious triumph in the simultaneous building of the great aqueduct at Pont Cysyllte (*q.v.*).

Long Eaton, Derbyshire □ MAP B

In Leopold Street are some of the lace factories that brought prosperity and expansion to this former village in the nineteenth century. Huge tenement factories of brick were built in this area in the last quarter of the nineteenth century, and here they flank the whole length of the road. They employed hundreds of workers who had previously known lace-making as a domestic craft, and turned it into a mass-production industry which brought an end to cottage lace-making here and in the villages of Hertfordshire and Buckinghamshire. For further information on lace-making, *see* Nottingham.

Longton, Staffordshire □ MAP B (*Stoke-on-Trent*)

The Gladstone Pottery, named after the statesman in honour of his visit to Burslem (*q.v.*) in 1863, is in Uttoxeter Road, and is now a working museum of the industry, with four preserved bottle ovens among the old brick buildings. The outer shell of these bottle-shaped kilns was called the 'hovel'. Within it was the oven, in which pottery was fired by heat distributed evenly from four fire-mouths. Modern methods have made these kilns redundant, and the many hundreds that once formed the Potteries' smoky skyline have nearly all disappeared. The processes of making pottery are demonstrated here, and the building complex includes an engine house and a saggar maker's shop, where fireclay cases were made for holding batches of pots during firing. Gladstone Pottery was featured in BBC TV's adaptation of Arnold Bennett's *Anna of the Five Towns*. The museum is open on working days throughout the year except Mondays in winter, and also on Sunday and some bank holiday afternoons. Tel: Stoke-on-Trent 319232.

Lothersdale, North Yorkshire × MAP B

At Dale End Mill, on a tributary of the River Aire, is a very large breastshot waterwheel built in 1861 to drive spinning and weaving machinery. It has a diameter of 44 feet and a width of 5 feet, and is made of cast iron, steel and wood, with 162 'buckets'. The mill was originally built for corn-milling.

The wheel is inside the building, as is usual in this part of the country.

Loughborough, Leicestershire □   MAP A

Taylors' Bell Foundry in Cobden Street is one of the only two old-established bell foundries in Britain, the other being in London's Whitechapel. John Taylor was an itinerant craftsman who came from Oxford in 1839 to recast the church bells at Loughborough. He liked the place, and set up permanent premises here later. Nearly a century and a half later, John Taylor and Company are still at work making bells that go all over the world, not only to churches and cathedrals, but to town halls, universities and other secular buildings. 'Great Paul' in St Paul's cathedral was cast by Taylors in 1881. The diameter of its mouth is 9½ feet and it weighs 17 tons – the largest bell in Britain. The age-old method of casting bells was to make a clay mould of the inside shape of the bell, then build up a layer of beeswax round it to the shape and thickness of the finished bell. Then a further clay mould was packed round this, and the whole thing was baked. The result was that the clay hardened and the wax melted, leaving a space between the inner core, called the 'crook', and the outer shell, called the 'cope'. Bell metal, an alloy of copper and tin, was then poured in and allowed to set before the clay was broken away to leave the bell ready for tuning and polishing. The bell foundry is not open to the public. In Queen's Park, however, the town's war memorial is a unique brick campanile housing 47 bells cast by Taylors in 1923.

Louth, Lincolnshire ≈   MAP B

The Louth Navigation runs north-east from the town and was opened in 1770 to ease the area's transport problems caused by bad roads. It linked Louth with the Humber estuary, and was used for commercial traffic until the First World War. There are 8 locks of unusual shape, having curved side-walls. Ticklepenny Lock is one of them, 1½ miles from the town. It raises the canal 7 feet.

Lower Slaughter, Gloucestershire ×   MAP A

At the upper end of this attractive Cotswold village, on the River Eye, is a former water mill now used as a bakery. Most unusually for this part of the country, it is built of red brick, though the tall chimney added to it is stone faced. The mill itself dates from early in the nineteenth century, and its waterwheel remains *in situ*.

Lowestoft, Suffolk ▲   MAP A

Fishing was the source of Lowestoft's livelihood from medieval times, and one or two of its old herring-curing houses survive, usually two- or three-storey buildings with shuttered upper floors and roof vents. One has the date 1676 on it.

Luton, Bedfordshire □   MAP A

Straw plaiting was a widespread cottage industry in and around the Chiltern Hills, but it has left scarcely a sign on the landscape, for it never became a factory industry. The museum at Wardown Park (north of the town centre) has tools and products of straw-plaiters and hat-makers, for the local expertise in straw plaiting made Luton the chief centre of the straw-hat industry. Plaiting seems to have been established originally at Luton Hoo, where James I settled French families brought to England by his mother, Mary Queen of Scots. The women and girls who worked long hours, often by candlelight, to supplement the meagre incomes their menfolk earned as farm labourers, used wheat straw cut by hand by the local farmers, to prevent the stems being broken by machinery.

Lyme Regis, Dorset ○   MAP A

Part of the harbour, known as the Cobb, remains from the late thirteenth or early fourteenth century, when the curved breakwater was built of large stones to construct a small harbour. Successive monarchs saw to its upkeep for its strategic value, until Lyme later developed into a trading port. Large-scale reconstruction took place in the eighteenth and nineteenth centuries, and among interesting buildings of the later period is a bonded warehouse built of the local limestone in 1830.

Lytham St Annes, Lancashire ×   MAP B

The breezy stretch of flat coastline on which Lytham stands relied on wind for power, and two restored windmills can be seen in the area, one here, the other at Thornton Cleveleys (*q.v.*). The one at Lytham St Annes is at East Beach, and was built around 1804. It is a white three-storey tower mill standing right on the sea front opposite St John's Church. Both were corn mills.

Macclesfield, Cheshire □   MAP B

Macclesfield is nothing if not a silk town. The first silk mill was built here in
1743 by Charles Roe, to whom there is a fitting monument in Christ
Church with a waterwheel among the carved reliefs. Several old mills
survive, but of equal interest is the industrial housing in so many of the
town's streets. In Paradise Street, in particular, weavers' workshops can be
seen on the top storeys of brick houses built early in the nineteenth century.
Frost's Mill at Park Green is a large four-storey brick building of 1785 in
characteristic factory style of the period, with the obligatory clock in the
gable (workers could have no excuses for being late for work). The mill was
powered originally by water, then converted to steam in 1811 and finally to
electricity in 1914. (A complete contrast in building style can be seen in
Commercial Road, where the 1883 frontage of the Arighi, Bianchi furniture showroom is of cast iron and glass.)

Maidenhead, Berkshire   =   MAP A

The viaduct carrying the railway over the Thames to the east of the town
centre was a typical *tour de force* of I.K. Brunel (*q.v.*) on his Great Western
Railway. Brunel designed the bridge of two semi-elliptical arches, each of
128 feet span, to be built of brick. They were the flattest brick arches ever
built at that time, and critics predicted their collapse under the weight of
trains, but the viaduct was built in 1838 and is still in use, carrying trains
from Paddington to the West Country. This is the bridge which Turner
painted in his famous 'Rain, Steam and Speed' in the National Gallery. A
lady traveller on the Exeter express told John Ruskin that she was in the
carriage from which Turner put his head out in a rainstorm to record the
scene mentally, and she saw the picture at the Royal Academy the next year,
in 1844. The artist was then nearly seventy. The dramatic diagonal
composition gives an impression of speed, but Turner humorously put a
hare on the track, running in front of the train, to show that the speed had
limits.

Maidstone, Kent   □   MAP A

Nineteenth-century paper mills remain at Maidstone in an area long
established as a paper-making centre. Springfield Mill, east of the town
centre, dates from the year of Trafalgar, and is said to be the earliest paper
mill powered by steam, having a Boulton and Watt beam engine installed
when it was opened for business. Hayle Mill was originally powered by a

waterwheel. Turkey Mill dates partly from the eighteenth century, having been taken over in 1740 by James Whatman, a name famous for high-quality papers, especially for artists. There has been a paper mill on its site since the Tudor period.

Manchester, Greater Manchester   =   MAP B

Manchester was in the vanguard of passenger railway development, and Liverpool Road Station was the original terminus of the Liverpool and Manchester Railway, and the earliest main line passenger station. It was built in 1829–30, but already by 1844 had been relegated to use as a goods station as railway development speeded ahead. Next to the station, with its two-storey stuccoed frontage, is the station master's house.

Mapledurham, Oxfordshire   ×   MAP A

In the grounds of Mapledurham House, where Alexander Pope visited the Blount sisters, is a brick and timber water mill, dating partly from the fifteenth century, with later additions, the oldest surviving mill on the River Thames. The wooden machinery is driven by an undershot waterwheel, and is operated for visitors on some afternoons in summer, producing

Mapledurham Mill

wholewheat flour by the traditional method between two pairs of mill-stones. Tel: Kidmore End 2642.

Marlow, Buckinghamshire   +   MAP A

The iron road bridge over the Thames, originally built in 1831, is a fine suspension bridge designed by William Tierney Clark, who subsequently built a similar but larger bridge across the Danube in Budapest. Clark's bridge at Marlow has a span of 271 feet. It has in its time been threatened with demolition as a bottleneck, but has been widened and is still happily intact.

Marston, Cheshire   □   MAP B

The Lion Salt Works, beside the Trent and Mersey Canal, is the only firm in Britain that still produces natural salt by open-pan boiling. The method produces salt crystals from brine pumped up from the salt beds by a steam engine. It is sold as additive-free block salt for preserving and other purposes – the form of salt which was common until the introduction of the 'free-running' salt produced in vacuum chambers. Visitors can see the works and methods in operation. The factory is open to the public seven days a week in the summer months; afternoons only. Tel: Northwich 2066.

Mary Tavy, Devon   △   MAP A

This was an important mining town on the western fringes of Dartmoor in the eighteenth and nineteenth centuries. The Wheal Friendship Mine produced lead, iron, copper and arsenic from right under the main street, and the production of arsenic here went on until 1925. Some remains of the plant are on the eastern outskirts of the village, while a mile to the north, off the A386, the National Trust preserves the former engine house of Wheal Betsy Mine, which produced lead, silver and zinc into the late 1870s, being known then as the Prince Arthur Consols mine. Engine house can be seen at any time.

Menai Strait, Gwynedd   +   MAP C

The Menai suspension bridge linking Anglesey with Holyhead was built by Thomas Telford (*q.v.*) from 1819–26 as the final part of his great work of re-aligning the road from London to Holyhead. He was forced to abandon his original plan for an arched bridge of cast iron by the need for ships to be able to pass through the strait, and he opted instead for a suspension bridge 100 feet above water level and with a span of 579 feet. It far exceeded anything of the kind done before anywhere in the world, and combined grace of design with several novel features in the construction. But it was a step into the unknown that caused Telford considerable anxiety despite his reputation for unruffled calmness in the face of difficulties. The chains for the bridge were cast at Upton Magna in Shropshire and thoroughly tested on a machine Telford devised for the purpose. There were 16 suspended chains, each weighing nearly 24 tons. Several modifications have been made to this bridge in the century and a half since its completion, but it remains basically the same bridge that Telford designed, and was one of the great civil-engineering achievements of the period.

Middlesbrough, Cleveland   +   MAP B

Transporter bridge at Middlesbrough

The world's largest transporter bridge, built in 1911, remains here spanning the Tees, and is a remarkable piece of engineering. It was built by the Cleveland Bridge and Engineering Co. to replace the ferry service across the river to Port Clarence and carries suspended cars below the gantry 160 feet above the river, to allow the passage of large vessels. The cars are

propelled electrically. The length of the bridge is 850 feet. *See also* Newport, Gwent, and Warrington.

Middleton-by-Wirksworth, Derbyshire   = MAP B

The Cromford and High Peak Railway was built 1825–31 to link the Cromford Canal at Cromford (*q.v.*) with the Peak Forest Canal at Whaley Bridge. The terminus at each end was connected to the line by a steep incline surmounted with the help of a stationary steam winding engine, and at Middleton Top the engine house survives complete with its engine, a Butterley double-beam engine of 1829 which has been restored to working order. It hauled wagons up a 1-in-8 slope. The engine may be seen on Sundays and on some Saturdays when it is operated. Tel: Matlock 3411.

Mistley, Essex ▲   MAP A

East of Manningtree on the Stour estuary, this village possesses a fine range of maltings built in the nineteenth century. The Old Maltings, disused since 1967, are two-storey buildings of the traditional type, in which barley was converted into malt for the brewing of ale. The malting business became concentrated in the south-eastern and eastern counties of England because that is where most of the country's barley was grown, and 'maltings', familiar by their long rows of windows and kilns with cowled tops, are most common in Essex, Suffolk and the eastern fringe of Hertfordshire. In the old method, barley grain was swollen by soaking in water for two or three days, then spread out on floors and exposed to air at a constant temperature to induce germination, which usually took two to three weeks. Then the grain was roasted in the kilns to produce malt for delivery to the breweries. The 'new' maltings at Mistley are multi-storey buildings of the late nineteenth century using more up-to-date methods, and are still working.

Moira, Leicestershire □   MAP A

The preserved blast furnace beside the Ashby Canal was built by Lord Moira, inheritor of the property of the powerful Hastings family, who had been mining coal here since the sixteenth century. The earl was one of the promoters of the canal, which was opened to traffic in 1794, and he continued to use it after his rivals had switched to the railway. The canal never actually reached Ashby-de-la-Zouch, which gave it its name, but it was a very successful commercial waterway. The large brick blast furnace was built with its tiers of arches at the beginning of the nineteenth century, and was producing iron for about a century and a half.

Monkwearmouth, Tyne & Wear   =   MAP B

The railway station in North Bridge Street is a notable example of the neo-classical style in railway architecture. It looks more like a museum, and indeed that is exactly what it now is. Built by John Dobson in 1848, it has tall Ionic columns with triangular pediment like a Greek temple. Open daily. Tel: Sunderland 7705.

Morwellham, Devon   ☆   MAP A

This village on the River Tamar 4 miles south-west of Tavistock was once a very busy port serving the largest copper mine in Europe, known as Great Consols. The miners worked for 14 shillings a week, making vast fortunes for the shareholders, chief of whom were the Russell family, who had acquired the land after the dissolution of the Benedictine abbey at Tavistock. A canal had been dug by French prisoners of war from what is now Dartmoor Prison, and it passed through a 2-mile-long tunnel to the hillside above the quay. Copper was brought by canal barge and inclined planes to the quay until, in the nineteenth century, the opening of the railway line to Plymouth affected its trade badly, and some 40 years later the mines themselves were exhausted. Arsenic refineries and lime kilns had been operated here, too. Now Morwellham Quay has been restored and developed as an open-air industrial museum, where visitors can see the docks, inclined planes and waterwheels, and go underground into one of the disused copper mines. The museum is open throughout the year. Tel: Tavistock 832766.

Mountsorrel, Leicestershire   △   MAP A

West of the village centre are vast quarries from which granite has been taken since Roman times. This Charnwood Forest granite is so hard that there was no known way of dressing it well enough for building purposes until the nineteenth century, but it was used for millstones and supplied road metal and kerbstones to London and other parts of England. The nineteenth-century village church is built of it.

Muirkirk, Strathclyde   +   MAP D

A cairn to the south of this coal-mining and iron-working town marks the
site of John Loudon McAdam's original works. One of the great early civil
engineers, and a contemporary of Thomas Telford (*q.v.*), McAdam revolu-
tionized road-making by his realization that a dry firm road surface would
support traffic without the necessity of such solid foundations as Telford
used. A tightly compacted surface of graded stones kept water at bay and
lasted a long time. McAdam's system, which involved his surveyors
checking the size of stones by passing them through a two-inch ring, was
soon adopted by the turnpike trusts. Spraying with tar was a later development in which McAdam himself had no part. There is a story that a
Hertfordshire man, George Allen, who made the metal rings for McAdam,
asked him what a stone-breaker was to do if he lost the ring. 'Why, George,'
McAdam replied, 'let him try the pieces in his mouth. If they go in they will
be small enough.'

Nailsworth, Gloucestershire   □   MAP A

The Cotswolds were at the forefront of woollen manufacturing in England
until the rise of factory industry gave precedence to Yorkshire. Nailsworth
was one of the important centres of the trade, and one of the ancient wool
town's pubs is still called the Clothier's Arms. North of the town centre on
the Stroud road, several old stone-built mill buildings survive, of which the
largest is Dunkirk Mills, dating partly from the eighteenth century. The
main range is of four storeys. Three waterwheels drove the machinery
here. The buildings are not open to the public, but Nailsworth and other
nearby Cotswold towns and villages, such as Chipping Campden, Pains-
wick and Uley, are rewarding places to visit for an impression of the wealth
of local clothiers who built themselves fine houses as well as fine churches
for their communities.

Nenthead, Cumbria   ☆   MAP B

On the bleak and barren Alston Moor, near the Durham border, is this
village built in the early nineteenth century for the miners employed by the
London Lead Company. The Quaker mine-owners could hardly avoid the
site's exposure to the ravages of moorland weather, but they provided for
the welfare of their employees, with sick pay and adult education schemes
that became models for other employers. What is now the 'over-sixties' rest
room' used to be the Mining Men's Reading Room. Relics of the

lead-mining and smelting industry are scattered on the moors in the vicinity. The industry declined before the century was out through competition from cheaper foreign lead.

Nether Alderley, Cheshire ×   MAP B

The Old Mill, in Congleton Road, is a sixteenth-century corn mill preserved in working order by the National Trust. It is a stone building with a big low-pitched and stone-flagged roof, and its power is provided by two overshot waterwheels. The mill remained in commercial use until the Second World War. It is open to the public during the afternoons in summer months, every day except Monday, and on Wednesday and Sunday afternoons in spring and autumn. Tel: Wilmslow 523012.

Nettlebed, Oxfordshire □   MAP A

At the village's eastern outskirts, surrounded now by a modern housing estate, a conical brick kiln is preserved. It stands like a phallic exhortation to the newly-weds living around it, but was a hive of industry once, dating possibly from the seventeenth century. Brick-making was an early industrial entrant into the Chiltern Hills, where there is no natural building stone except flint, and it was in the fifteenth century that brick works first appeared at Nettlebed, to establish a local business that lasted for five hundred years.

Newcastle-on-Tyne, Tyne & Wear =   MAP B

Of the five bridges crossing the Tyne at Newcastle, none is more famous than the High Level Bridge built 1845–9 by Robert Stephenson (*q.v.*). It was a daring piece of engineering – a railway bridge constructed of iron arches between stone piers, with a road bridge and footpaths suspended below the arches. It takes the railway line into the city's Central Station, itself a notable piece of railway building, designed by John Dobson, the architect who was responsible for so much of Newcastle's new central stylishness in the nineteenth century. The station was built in 1850.

Newcastle-on-Tyne, Tyne & Wear +   MAP B

Between the High Level Bridge (*q.v.*) and the New Tyne Bridge of 1928 is the Swing Bridge, which was built in 1876 to replace the only river crossing that was here before Stephenson's railway bridge. There had been a bridge

since Roman times, and some remains of a medieval one can still be seen. The value of Newcastle's shipping industry in the nineteenth century made it necessary for large ships to pass up the river, and the low stone bridge of 1771 was demolished to make way for the Swing Bridge built by Armstrongs, and at that time the largest of its kind in the world. It is 281 feet long and weighs nearly 1,500 tons. It was originally operated by steam-powered hydraulic pumps, but is now driven electrically.

THOMAS NEWCOMEN

The inventor of the 'atmospheric engine', which was one of the greatest technological advances in modern history, was born at Dartmouth (*q.v.*) in 1663. Thomas Newcomen became a blacksmith and an ironmonger, and it was in 1705 that, in partnership with Thomas Savery and John Colley, he patented the first engine which made use of steam as a motive power. The revolutionary principle was the introduction of a piston into the cylinder, which was pushed up by steam pressure to raise one end of a rocking beam. The piston then fell again under atmospheric pressure to raise the other end of the beam. The immediate application of this engine was in pumping water out of mine workings, which had often become so badly flooded that it was impossible for them to be worked, and pumps driven by waterwheels were unequal to the huge drainage problems. So Newcomen in the short term was the saviour of the mining industry. But in the long term he opened the way to the great revolution in industry that came with the advances on his original idea, made by such as James Watt and Richard Trevithick (*qq.v.*). Newcomen died in 1729, when his engines were coming into increasing use all over Europe as well as in Britain, and soon in America too, but he had gained little financial advantage from his invention. His house in Dartmouth was demolished when a new road was made in 1864, and the fact that the road is named Newcomen Road is no compensation for the loss of a house that would have been holy ground for today's industrial enthusiasts. There is a monument to Newcomen, however, in the park of Bayard's Cove, Dartmouth.

New Lanark, Strathclyde ☆   MAP D

Late in the eighteenth century a Glasgow industrialist, David Dale, built a cotton mill here in collaboration with Arkwright (*q.v.*), and around it built a model village for his workers. In 1797, Robert Owen (*q.v.*) met Dale's daughter, Anne Caroline Dale, whom he later married, and subsequently took over the New Lanark Mills, which employed a thousand people.

Here Owen set about the great social reforms which made New Lanark for a time one of the most celebrated places in Britain; he improved both the working and the living conditions of those on whose labour he depended, and proposed a system of universal co-operation in industry in place of the misery of exploitation. The old mills, houses, school and other buildings dating from Robert Owen's time are preserved, and there is an exhibition centre in a former counting house.

Newnham Bridge, Hereford & Worcester ✕ MAP A

Newnham Mill, on the River Rea near the busy road junction, is an eighteenth-century water-powered corn mill which has been restored to full working order, its machinery driven by an undershot wheel of fifteen-foot diameter. The mill can be seen working at weekends and bank holidays in the summer months. Tel: Newnham Bridge 445.

Newport, Gwent + MAP C

Crossing the River Usk near the docks is one of the only four transporter bridges built in Britain. Their purpose was to span rivers without hindering navigation, by supporting a beam high above the water level on two towers, and carrying goods across in vehicles suspended from the beam on cables. The Newport bridge was built in 1906, the second of the British transporter bridges, and it is still used.

Newport, Isle of Wight ☐ MAP A

North-east of the town centre is a large factory built in 1827 for the lace manufacturers Freeman and Nunn. The firm came here from the Midlands, where new lace-making machinery was threatened by the Luddite riots (see also Tiverton). The factory is a three-storey building of yellow brick. It was used as a lace factory until 1877, and is now government property. Nearby is the hospital, originally built as a House of Industry, or workhouse, around 1770.

Newport Pagnell, Buckinghamshire + MAP A

The cast-iron bridge carrying the main road over the River Ouzel or Lovat south of the town dates from 1810, and is an interesting example of early iron bridge construction. Called Tickford Bridge, it is said to be the oldest iron bridge in Britain still in constant use. Further speculation ascribes its basic design to Thomas Paine, author of *The Rights of Man* (*see also* Sunderland). It was actually Henry Provis who built this single-span bridge, but the construction method of openwork voussoirs bound together with iron straps was patented by Rowland Burdon, a Sunderland M.P.

Newton, Northumberland ▲   MAP B

The Hunday National Tractor and Farm Museum at this location near Corbridge has Europe's finest collection of vintage tractors, as well as stationary steam engines and other agricultural machinery. An early eighteenth-century water mill has also been re-erected at the site, with a twenty-foot wheel driving two pairs of millstones. Open daily throughout the year. Tel: Stocksfield 842553.

Newtown, Powys ☆   MAP C

The birthplace of Robert Owen (*q.v.*) was formerly an important weaving town, and in Commercial Street there is a Textile Museum, once a workshop. Exhibits include hand looms and later machinery. There is also a museum dedicated to the life and work of Robert Owen, on the site of his birthplace, above the Midland Bank. Both museums are open on weekdays only in the summer months.

Northampton, Northamptonshire ☆   MAP A

In Bridge Street is a Museum of Leathercraft, at the heart of the region associated with the boot and shoe industry. The museum exhibits the uses of leather throughout history, with a fine collection of leather craftsman-made objects (not just footwear). The museum is open on weekdays throughout the year. Tel: Northampton 34881.

Northwich, Cheshire △   MAP B

The 'wich' name ending is a clue to an ancient industry for which Cheshire is famous – salt mining. Northwich, Middlewich and Nantwich, as well as Droitwich in Hereford and Worcester, were all known to the Romans for their salt deposits, and several ancient routes across Britain are known as 'salt ways' because salt was carried on them in trains of packhorses to the far corners of the kingdom. The salt beds lie beneath the rock known to geologists as Keuper Sandstone, and mining was the early method of extracting it. One firm still mines salt at Winsford. It was found later that if bore holes were sunk into the deposits and water circulated in them, the solution could be pumped up and the salt extracted by evaporation, and this is what is done at Marston (*q.v.*). The effects of mining can be seen around Northwich, where the formation of large pools or 'flashes' is due to mining subsidence. In London Road there is a Salt Museum with exhibits on the history and techniques of this essential industry, in a building that was once the local workhouse. Open during afternoons daily except Monday. Tel: Northwich 41331.

Norwich, Norfolk   +   MAP A

The old part of Norwich is tucked into a bend in the River Wensum, and as the city expanded, many bridges were built to carry its roads over the river. One of them carries Coslany Street north from St Laurence's Church, and is a cast-iron bridge of 1804, making it one of the earliest surviving iron bridges in Britain, built a quarter of a century after Shropshire's famous pioneer at Ironbridge (*q.v.*).

Nottingham, Nottinghamshire   □   MAP B

Around Stoney Street (south-east of city centre near St Mary's Church) is a commercial complex built in the nineteenth century, occupying a considerable part of the medieval town's former area, and now known as the Lace Market. It consists mostly of plain four-storey brick warehouses with a few more ornate buildings among them. Nottingham's lace industry arose from attempts to bring to hand-lace-making the kind of mechanization that Midlands manufacturers had brought to hosiery knitting. In the second half of the eighteenth century some progress was made, but it was the invention of the bobbin net machine by John Heathcoat (*see* Tiverton) in 1808 that provided the foundation for mechanical lace-making. By 1885 Nottingham had over 2,000 machines at work in steam-powered factories, and 10 per cent of the whole county's population was employed in the lace industry. The enormous increase in the demand for lace was largely due to the fashion for lace curtains which came at the same time as a huge house-building programme, and buyers came from home and abroad to negotiate their deals in the Lace Market.

O RICHARD OASTLER

When the Industrial Revolution brought huge woollen mills powered by steam to the towns of Yorkshire's West Riding, there were many unfortunate social consequences. Thousands of insanitary back-to-back houses were built to get as many as inhumanly possible into every acre of land to accommodate the legions of workers. During the nineteenth century, Leeds increased its population from 53,000 to nearly half a million, and Bradford's growth rate was even greater. One of the worst effects of massive manufacturing industry was the employment of young children in the factories for up to fifteen hours a day, when the huge slump in hand-loom weaving forced parents to live off their children. Children employed by such as William Douglas at his cotton mill in Salford were often taken from the workhouse at six or seven years old and worked for long hours, and were sometimes so ill-treated that they committed suicide. Douglas's mill was known as the 'Cripple Factory' because children became deformed by the work they were forced to do. Richard Oastler was a leading campaigner against those who employed children. He was born in Leeds in 1789 and trained as an architect, but by 1830 had taken over the fight against child abuses from Robert Owen (*q.v.*), and conducted a vigorous campaign for a ten-hour day, which only succeeded in 1847 with the passing of the Ten Hour Bill limiting the working hours of all those aged up to eighteen. Oastler was a hero of the Yorkshire working classes, and his statue stands in Bradford's Rawson Square with two children. He died in 1861.

Oldham, Greater Manchester □　　　　MAP B

Oldham was the scene of a great building boom in the second half of the nineteenth century, and many ordinary working folk bought shares in the great cotton industry that gave rise to it. The Oldham Stock Exchange developed out of a new class of capitalists not portrayed in the industrial scenarios of Marx and Engels. The small town that had a dozen mills and a population of 10,000 at the beginning of the nineteenth century had grown by 1890 to a place of 130,000 people and 265 mills, and was called 'the greatest cotton-spinning town in the world'. Though many mills have been either demolished or converted to other uses, the great buildings still dominate the town. They are mostly of brick, unlike the woollen mills of Yorkshire, which are nearly always of stone.

Otley, West Yorkshire ☆　　　　MAP B

In the churchyard of All Saints, a monument stands to the men killed during the construction of the nearby Bramhope railway tunnel in 1845–9. It consists of a scale model of the tunnel's castellated northern portal. The tunnel was built by the Leeds and Thirsk Railway, and is a little over two miles in length. The towers of ventilating shafts can be seen above its course.

Ottery St Mary, Devon ✕ MAP A

A five-storey brick mill at the western outskirts of the little town was built in 1790 as a serge mill, powered by a waterwheel driven by the River Otter (the waterwheel is no longer in use). The venture was unsuccessful, and thirty-three years later the mill became a silk factory. It is now occupied by an engineering company, and is not open to the public, but its most interesting feature is outside and can be seen from beside the millstream. It is a rare circular weir through which water by-passing the wheel tumbles into a tunnel beneath the mill on its return to the river.

Outwood, Surrey ✕ MAP A

The windmill in full working order on the heath is a post mill of 1665, the earliest mill still operable, though its machinery dates mainly from the nineteenth century. The weatherboarded top was originally supported by the timber trestle, which has since been enclosed within a brick round-house. The mill can be visited at weekends.

Over Haddon, Derbyshire △ MAP B

West of the village in Lathkilldale are remains of the lead-mining industry once so important in the Peak District. The remains of engine houses and mining shafts are found over a wide area in this region, as well as 'rakes' – long fissures stretching for miles across the landscape, where miners extracted ore from narrow veins in the carboniferous limestone. Here, as well as an engine house and other works, is Mandale Sough, a drainage channel one mile long which took twenty-three years to dig. By the time it was finished, the workings had gone lower than the levels it was meant to drain.

ROBERT OWEN

Born in 1771 at Newtown (*q.v.*), Owen was the son of an ironmonger and one of seven children. He left home at the age of ten and went to London, then to Stamford, where he became apprentice to a draper and educated himself in his spare time. After a brief return to London, he went to Manchester, and was soon in business building spinning machines for the cotton mills, from which he graduated to becoming a mill owner himself at New Lanark (*q.v.*) with a thousand employees. Here he put into practice the ideas of social justice expounded in his book *A New View of Society*, and became a nationally known figure. His chief concerns were with the conditions of labour and education of the working classes, and he was the instigator of the Factory Act of 1819, which prohibited the employment in textile mills of children under ten, and reduced working hours for those under eighteen. The Bill took four years to get through Parliament, during which time Owen was subjected to abuse by those who opposed it, and on his deathbed in 1858, a clergyman who came (needlessly) to offer him the consolations of religion asked him if he regretted having wasted his life in fruitless efforts! Owen was buried in the churchyard at Newtown, and there is a statue of him in the town's memorial park.

P Papplewick, Nottinghamshire ✕ MAP B

North-east of the village, off the A60, is the Papplewick Pumping Station, which could supply water to Nottingham at the rate of three million gallons a day. The water was raised by two rotative beam engines built by James Watt (*q.v.*) and Co. in 1884, which are still *in situ*. The building itself is quite stylish, both inside and out, with decorative tiling and stained-glass windows, and an ornamental pond in front. It is preserved by a trust and can be visited during weekends in the summer months.

Pendeen, Cornwall △ MAP A

The Geevor Tin Mine still operates, which is rare, and maintains a museum, open to the public during the summer months, and showing the history of tin mining in the region. The tin treatment plant can also be visited by prior arrangement. Tel: Penzance 788662.

Pitstone, Buckinghamshire ✕ MAP A

Near the village is a post mill, restored and owned by the National Trust, and reckoned to be one of the oldest surviving windmills in the British Isles, having the date 1627 carved on one of its interior timbers. The mill was operated commercially as a corn mill until 1902, when a freak storm did extensive damage to its structure, but the interior wooden machinery, driving two pairs of millstones, is original, and provides a fascinating glimpse of the millwright's craftsmanship. The mill is usually open on Sunday afternoons in the summer months.

Plymouth, Devon   ○   MAP A

On Plymouth Hoe is the so-called Smeaton's Tower. The engineer John
Smeaton was the builder of the third Eddystone Lighthouse. The first two
lighthouses on the site had been destroyed by storm and fire, and Smeaton
built his lighthouse of granite and Portland (*q.v.*) stone in 1759. It stood for
123 years before being partly dismantled because the rock on which it stood
was insecure. The present lighthouse, which can be seen from here on a
clear day, fourteen miles out to sea, was substituted for it in 1882, and the
upper part of Smeaton's building was re-erected here as a monument to
Smeaton himself, while the lower part still stands out on the reef beside the
new lighthouse.

Pont Cysyllte, Clwyd   ≈   MAP C

The aqueduct carrying the Shropshire Union Canal across the valley of the
River Dee near Llangollen is possibly the *magnum opus* of that man of
engineering masterpieces, Thomas Telford (*q.v.*). Previous canal
aqueducts had been low affairs with channels of puddled clay supported on
Pont Cysyllte   brick arches. This would not do at Pont Cysyllte, as the aqueduct had to
aqueduct   cross the valley at a high level and the weight of water in its clay bed on

massive masonry supports would be too great for the foundations. Telford abandoned all precedents and built in 1805 an aqueduct of cast iron supported on 18 stone piers 121 feet above the river. It is over 1,000 feet in length, with a towpath alongside, and is a spectacular sight both from below and from the bridge itself (which you can walk). George Borrow and his guide were not the only visitors to feel dizzy as they gazed down from it. The aqueduct is not only the most breathtaking of all canal works, but one of the greatest structural engineering achievements of any kind. A sort of prototype for the cast-iron channel was carried out simultaneously by Telford at Longdon-upon-Tern (q.v.).

Pontypridd, Mid-Glamorgan   +   MAP C

At the centre of the town is an elegant masonry bridge crossing the River Taff. It was built in 1756 by a local stonemason, William Edwards. It was his third attempt, and he reduced the inward and upward thrust of the bridge by piercing the spandrels (the triangular spaces between the crossing and its supports) with three cylindrical tunnels at each end. The bridge has a span of 140 feet and is 35 feet above the river. At the time of its completion it was thought to be the longest single-span bridge in the world.

Porthmadog, Gwynedd   =   MAP C

The town is the headquarters of the Ffestiniog narrow-gauge railway, which has its terminus and museum at the Harbour Station. The line was opened in 1836 to carry slate from quarries at Blaenau Ffestiniog (q.v.) to the port. Its gauge is narrower than that of the Tal-y-llyn (q.v.) at 1 foot 11½ inches. At the end of the nineteenth century the line was transporting 140,000 tons of slate a year, but it also ran passenger services on the scenic route, beginning with a daily train at 5.25 a.m. to take quarrymen to work. The railway closed in 1946 with the decline of the slate industry, and lay derelict for 8 years before the Ffestiniog Railway Society began to restore locomotives and rescue track and rolling stock from rust and undergrowth which had consumed it. The line is now open again, mainly for the tourist traffic, and it claims to be the world's oldest narrow-gauge passenger railway.

Porth-y-Nant, Gwynedd   △   MAP C

The deserted village of ruined houses at Porth-y-Nant grew up originally in the nineteenth century when quarry owners exploited the local granite

cliffs to satisfy a demand for the material as building stone – especially in
Liverpool. Workers came from Cornwall as well as local areas to work as
quarrymen, and terraces of cottages were built to house them. But the
demand for the granite dried up in the present century, and the workers
and their families departed, leaving a ghost village. The quarry workings
are on the cliff above the former settlement.

Portland, Dorset △   MAP A

The bleak and treeless 'Isle' of Portland, which is in fact a peninsula
connected to the mainland by the natural ridge of shingle known as Chesil
Bank, is a solid block of limestone 4 miles long by 2 miles wide. 'Its soile',
wrote the Elizabethan antiquary John Leland, with delightful English
understatement, 'is sumwhat stony.' Portland stone has been quarried for
many centuries, and much of central London has been built out of great
holes in the ground here. Sir Christopher Wren used 50,000 tons to
rebuild St Paul's Cathedral. To facilitate transportation of the stone by sea
to London and other destinations, several jetties were built around the
peninsula's eastern coast and Durdle Pier, east of the 'island's' central
urban area of Easton, is the only one surviving from the eighteenth century.
Quarrying continues to be the chief industry of the place, for Portland
stone is still one of the world's finest building stones, fine-grained and
easily worked, and lending itself particularly well to 'monumental'
architecture.

Portree, Skye ○   MAP D

The harbour at Portree was originally built by Thomas Telford (*q.v.*) in
1819, during his great work of improving communications in the Highlands. A row of stone cottages built by Telford also remains here.

Portsmouth, Hampshire ○   MAP A

The world's first dry dock was built here in the reign of Henry VII, and
Nelson's flagship at Trafalgar, *HMS Victory*, is now moored in it as part of
the Royal Navy Museum. This is the only part of the naval dockyards at
Portsmouth which is open to the public – on weekdays and Sunday
afternoons throughout the year.

Port Sunlight, Merseyside ☆　　　　　　　MAP B

The first Lord Leverhulme's famous industrial settlement was begun in 1888 to provide comfortable housing in pleasant surroundings for the workers at the Lever Brothers soap works, now the largest in the world. The original Sunlight Soap was made to William Hesketh Lever's own formula from vegetable oils, and its success brought rapid expansion of the business. The model village was a great advance on anything of the kind done before. Groups of cottages were arranged in a spacious setting round little greens. Four hundred houses had been built by the turn of the century. The estate had a church, inn (originally a 'temperance hotel'), recreation hall, fire station, school, shop and a sunken garden called the Dell. Viscount Leverhulme was a Liberal M.P. who had campaigned for old-age pensions and believed in shorter working hours and the right of workers to withhold their labour. But there was opposition to his Port Sunlight scheme from the unions. No one could feel any sense of independence in this paternalistic community, where the workers' life styles and morals were 'looked after' in the same way as their material needs, unlike the Cadburys' village at Bournville (*q.v.*). After the death of his wife, Lord Leverhulme built the Lady Lever Art Gallery as a memorial to her. Among other fine works there is a portrait of Thomas Telford (*q.v.*) by Raeburn. Both the factory and the village can be toured by arrangement. Tel: Liverpool 644 9444.

Preston, Lancashire □　　　　　　　　　MAP B

In New Hall Lane is Centenary Mill, interesting as one of the new generation of large factory buildings that used up-to-date structural techniques at the end of the nineteenth century, in order to accommodate larger and heavier machinery on several floors. The mill was built by the famous firm of Horrocks in 1895, a hundred years after John Horrocks had opened his first mill at Preston. Centenary Mill has concrete floors and beams of rolled steel, and as the exterior walls of brick do not have to bear so much of the mill's load, more of their area could be given to windows to let in more light. The mill is not open to the public.

Preston Brook, Cheshire ≈　　　　　　　MAP B

This is an interesting canal settlement at the junction of the Bridgewater Canal with the Trent and Mersey, and the site of a tunnel begun by James Brindley (*q.v.*) and completed in 1775 after his death. It is 1,239 yards long and was one of the first long canal tunnels in Britain.

Prestongrange, Lothian ✕   MAP D

Between Musselburgh and Prestonpans is the Prestongrange Colliery
Historical Site, devoted to the Scottish coal industry. The star attraction
here is a Cornish beam engine, built by Harveys of Hayle (*q.v.*) in 1874,
which was used for 80 years to pump water from the mine. The massive
beam, 33 feet long, weighs 30 tons.

Priddy, Somerset △   MAP A

About a mile to the east of the village are some remains of the once
extensive lead-mining industry of the Mendip Hills. The pub at the nearby
crossroads is still called The Miner's Arms. Foundations and remains of
furnaces mark the site of the former St Cuthbert Lead Works which was in
operation until just before the 1914–18 war. Here the mined ore was
converted into metallic lead by purification and smelting. The old process
of removing impurities was called 'buddling', and remains of buddle floors
can be seen at this site. The crushed ore was flowed into the buddle with
water, and the heavy metal sank into a central trough while the residue was
washed away.

Princetown, Devon △   MAP A

Her Majesty's Prison at Princetown on Dartmoor is an industrial monument of sorts although, naturally, public interest in it is not encouraged. It
was Thomas Tyrwhitt, an Essex man who owned granite quarries on the
moor, who proposed to the government the building of a prison or barracks
for the French prisoners of war who were lying in rotten and overcrowded
hulks at Plymouth. The plan was eventually accepted. Tyrwhitt's own
quarries would supply the granite, of course, and he laid the foundation
stone in 1806. The job was a nightmare for the building contractors, more
than one of whom went bankrupt, but in three years the first prisoners were
moved in. Tyrwhitt himself had founded Prince's Town, named in honour
of his friend the Prince of Wales, and in due course he was knighted for his
enterprise. He built a railway line to the town from Plymouth, and when all
the prisoners of war had left Dartmoor, he suggested using the prison for
convicts, who would work as stone-breakers, helping to clear the ground
for his grandiose and abortive scheme to put large areas of Dartmoor
under cultivation. Carved in the granite over the grim portal of Dartmoor
Prison is the inscription *Parcere subjectis* – Pity the Humbled. For well over
a century, convicts on Dartmoor have carried out the soul-destroying

work of stone-breaking to supply granite for road-building and other purposes.

Pumpsaint, Dyfed △   MAP C

Half a mile south east of the village, on the National Trust's Dolaucothi estate, are the remains of the Ogofau gold mines, worked at least as long ago as Roman times and possibly earlier. Sporadic working has occurred since then, particularly at the end of the nineteenth century and for a few years before the Second World War, but returns have not justified the investment. Visitors can see the remains of Roman open-cast mines and the shafts where underground mining was done. Gold ornaments and Roman pottery have been found here, and there was a fort nearby to guard the imperial interest. Wooden waterwheels were built to drain the galleries, and stone-lined aqueducts carried water to the site for washing the ore. Other gold mines have been worked in the hills around Dolgellau, notably at Gwynfynydd, where the Morgan Gold Mining Company took £35,000 worth of gold in the late nineteenth century. Surface remains visible at this mine include a strong-room near one of the adit entrances. The yield in Welsh gold has always been relatively low, but one of the traditions which grew out of its discovery and exploitation is that royal wedding rings are always made of Welsh gold.

Pymore, Cambridgeshire ✕   MAP A

Near this village in the Fens, beside the New Bedford River, there is a pumping station, originally built about 1830 for a Watt beam engine to raise water from the River Lark to flow into the Great Ouse, as part of the continuing operation to keep the Bedford Level free of flooding. There is a plaque on the wall with the apt inscription:

> These fens have oft' times been by water drowned,
> Science a remedy in water found.
> The power of steam she said shall be employed
> The destroyer by itself shall be destroyed.

R Rainhill, Merseyside =   MAP B

The railway station is an historic site in the development of railway transport. In October 1829 a competition was held on a mile and a half of level track here to test the potential of steam locomotives for passenger trains. Known as the Rainhill Trials, the competition was spread over several days and was watched by 10,000 spectators. The Liverpool and Manchester Railway offered a prize of £500 for the locomotive which could best meet the company's conditions, which involved pulling power, speed and boiler pressure. The winner was, as everyone knows, Stephenson's (*q.v.*) 'Rocket', which successfully met all the requirements.

Ravenscar, North Yorkshire △   MAP B

A Geology Trail starting from the road junction near Raven Hall Hotel reveals extensive quarrying remains where alum was extracted during the nineteenth century. Alum was used as a mordant – a fixative for textile dyes – and in the two huge pits known as the Peak and Brown quarries the extracted shale was calcined before being transported to Sandsend, near Whitby, where it was shipped from a specially built wharf.

Reading, Berkshire ☆   MAP A

The Museum of English Rural Life in Whiteknights Park was set up by Reading University, and has a fine collection of agricultural tools and wagons, and exhibits on other rural crafts and industries. Open Tuesday to Saturday only. Tel: Reading 875123.

Redruth, Cornwall △   MAP A

The Tolgus Tin Works, a mile to the north of the town on Portreath Road, is a museum of tin mining as well as a working site. The history of the industry is illustrated, and visitors can see the only remaining set of working Cornish 'stamps', driven by a waterwheel to crush the ores of tin oxide prior to smelting. The process of 'streaming' tin is shown, whereby ore is extracted from the rock by running water, which washes waste sediment away and leaves the heavier metal behind. One of the by-products of tin mining is arsenic, and at the Tolgus Works is a 'calciner' in which ore was roasted in a furnace to give off arsenic. The works are open to visitors from April to October. Tel: Redruth 5171.

Reedham, Norfolk ✕   MAP A

The Berney Arms Mill, 3 miles north-east of the village, is the tallest mill in Britain built for drainage purposes, being 7 storeys and 70 feet high. As drainage mills were much influenced by Dutch models, this is a smock mill, which is basically the same as a tower mill in its operation, but has an octagonal tower of weatherboarded walls and in the Netherlands is called a 'spinnekop'. This one was built in 1840 and is in the care of the Department of the Environment. It is open to the public, but there is no road access. It can be reached by boat or from Berney Arms Station on the railway line between Reedham and Great Yarmouth.

Rhondda, Mid-Glamorgan △   MAP C

The town of Rhondda, seven miles north-west of Pontypridd, is at the centre of the river valley whose name has become synonymous with coal mining. There are actually two Rhonddas – Rhondda Fawr and Rhondda Fach – which meet at Pontypridd. It is one of the grimmest and most tragic industrial landscapes in Britain, despite much recent redevelopment. Welsh coal had been mined on a small scale as early as the Tudor period, and it was already a big industry by the seventeenth century, but its exploitation in the Industrial Revolution made vast profits for mine owners at the expense of a variety of living things. Shafts of unprecedented depth were sunk in the area in the nineteenth century, down which men, women, children, ponies and canaries were sent to work in appalling conditions – the canaries to give warning of the presence of gas which was responsible for many disasters and killed huge numbers of miners: 145 at Risca in 1860; 178 at Ferndale in 1867; 439 at Senghennydd in 1913. Men who did not lose their lives in mine disasters were liable to die relatively young from respiratory diseases or from cholera epidemics which hit the cramped and insanitary housing put up by the mine owners for their workers. Where ponies could not be used to haul coal along narrow passages, children of six or seven years of age were sent instead, to work as carters on twelve-hour shifts. Some of these evils were ended by Lord Shaftesbury's Act of 1842 forbidding the employment of women and children in coal mines. The scene today is largely one of dereliction, with terraces of brick houses clinging to the hillsides with slag-heaps above and disused colliery buildings and pithead winding gear below, where the small individual mines that gave life to their communities have been replaced by larger and more economical modern pits. The National Museum of Wales at Cardiff (*q.v.*) has important exhibits on the coal-mining industry.

Ridsdale, Northumberland □   MAP B

The ruins of an engine house and other remains of a short-lived iron works can be seen here, dating from the mid-nineteenth century. The engine house contained two steam blowing engines.

Roade, Northamptonshire =   MAP A

The railway line west of the village passes through a deep cutting made in 1834 for the London and Birmingham Railway. It is 1½ miles long and 55 feet deep. It was necessitated by Robert Stephenson's (*q.v.*) insistence on gentle gradients, and involved 800 navvies, miners and masons in a complicated and dangerous job of blasting limestone and removing a million cubic yards of earth and rock from a site which proved to be waterlogged and needed steam engines to pump continuously for over a year before the earthworks could be completed.

Rochdale, Greater Manchester +   MAP B

The March Bridge carrying Gipsy Lane over the Rochdale Canal south-west of the town at Castleton is believed to be the first skew-arch bridge built with winding courses of stone. The canal was opened in 1804 and the engineer, William Jessop, was probably responsible for this pioneering road bridge.

Rosedale, North Yorkshire △   MAP B

North-west of the village called Rosedale Abbey on the North York Moors are the remains of ironstone mines and batteries of calcining kilns, in which the ore was purified. The calcining process removed water and carbon dioxide and other impurities from the ore by roasting it with coal. The arched kilns date from the 1860s, when a branch railway brought modern transport to the local industry which had previously used packhorses to carry its ore to Pickering, twelve miles away. Rosedale had been involved in iron making since at least as early as the thirteenth century, when the monks of Byland Abbey worked the deposits. The miners themselves travelled up the valley to their works on donkeys before the railway came, as they had done since the industry began in medieval times. The railway was dismantled long ago, and its course is now a public right of way which can be used to reach the workings.

Rotherfield Greys, Oxfordshire ☆   MAP A

At the Tudor mansion Greys Court, north of the village and now owned by the National Trust, there is a well house containing a donkey wheel, used from the sixteenth century until the First World War to draw water from the well, which is 200 feet deep. The timber wheel is 19 feet in diameter, and, as the donkey trod it, it lowered an empty bucket and raised a full one at the same time. This is the largest surviving donkey wheel in England. The grounds and well-house are open on some summer afternoons. Tel: Rotherfield Greys 529.

Rowlands Gill, Tyne & Wear ☐   MAP B

At this location by the River Derwent is preserved a range of nineteenth-century coke ovens. Coke was produced by burning coal starved of oxygen to drive off the gases, and has remained an important by-product of the coal industry, though now produced by more sophisticated methods.

Ruddington, Nottinghamshire ☆   MAP B

An ensemble of stocking-knitters' cottages and early workshops has been converted into a most interesting museum of the framework knitting industry. Wooden hand frames can be seen in operation here, and there are documents and photographs on the history of this important East Midlands industry, as well as examples of early products. The museum is in Chapel Street, and is open by appointment. Tel: Nottingham 213287 or 211858.

Ryhope, Tyne & Wear ✕   MAP B

One of the most distinctive examples of industrial architecture in the north-east of England, the Ryhope Pumping Station was built in 1868 by the Sunderland and South Shields Water Company. It is an ornate two-storey gabled building designed to accommodate two rotative compound beam engines built by Hawthorns of Newcastle. The engines remained in service for nearly a century, and are now preserved by a trust in full working order. Open during afternoons at weekends and bank holidays from April to September.

S St Albans, Hertfordshire ✕   MAP A

Kingsbury Mill at the foot of Fishpool Street dates back to the sixteenth century, when it was part of Sir Francis Bacon's estate of Gorhambury. The site was probably occupied by a mill in Saxon times, for Kingsbury was a royal borough before the Norman Conquest. The present building is of brick and timber-frame construction with weatherboarded gables added in the eighteenth century. The mill was in commercial use as a flour mill until the 1960s, with three pairs of millstones driven by an undershot iron waterwheel, powered by the River Ver which gave the Roman town of Verulamium its name. The restored mill is now a museum with its machinery intact, and is open daily. Tel: St Albans 53323.

St Fagans, South Glamorgan ☆ MAP C

At the western outskirts of Cardiff, St Fagans is the home of the Welsh Folk Museum, the most interesting section of which, in the present context, is the outdoor museum, although an indoor gallery contains a fine collection of agricultural machinery. Re-erected farmhouses and exhibits of rural crafts and industry outside include the Esgair Moel woollen mill, brought from Llanwrtyd and in renewed operation here. The mill was originally built about 1760, and is powered by a waterwheel. The museum is open throughout the year except Sunday mornings and winter bank holidays. Tel: Cardiff 569441.

St Helens, Merseyside ≈ MAP B

The first truly industrial canal in Britain was financed mainly by Liverpool manufacturers to link the St Helens coalfield with the Mersey. The St Helens Canal was opened to traffic in 1751. Off the A58 east of the town are the so-called Old Double Locks, which were the first staircase locks in the country, built in 1758. The canal remained in commercial use until 1940, but much of it has now disappeared in area redevelopment.

St Helens, Merseyside □ MAP B

The glass-making industry of St Helens had its origins in vast local deposits of ideal sand for the purpose, and developed into the chief centre of the business in the second half of the eighteenth century. In 1773 the British Plate Glass Company built a casting hall at the Ravenhead Glass Works, which was reputedly the largest factory under one roof in Britain at the time. What remains of this is now part of the Pilkington works, where there is a fine museum of the glass industry. The housing explosion of the Industrial Revolution created a huge demand for sheet glass, which is produced by the fusion of sand, sodium carbonate and limestone. The sand has to be free of iron, otherwise the glass turns green. The mixture of raw materials is called 'frit' and it is melted at temperatures of up to 1600°C. The fabrication of sheet glass was done until relatively recent years by pouring the molten glass through water-cooled rollers on to an 'annealing lehr', where it was cooled slowly and toughened. Then it was cut to size, ground and polished. In 1959, however, Sir Alistair Pilkington introduced the 'float glass' method, in which the molten glass is floated across a bath of liquid tin, and this eliminates the time-consuming processes of grinding and polishing, producing clear sheets of brilliant glass. The Pilkington Glass Museum, in Prescot Road, is open daily on weekdays and during afternoons at weekends and most bank holidays. Tel: St Helens 28882.

Salford, Greater Manchester △   MAP B

At Buile Hill Park, in Eccles Old Road, is the Salford Science Museum, devoted to local industries and having a particularly good section on coal mining. There is a reproduction of a mine, and exhibits include a good collection of miners' lamps. The early lamps had open flames which could ignite inflammable gases and cause explosions, through which a great many lives were lost. The famous safety lamp invented by Humphry Davy in 1816 had its flame enclosed by a fine wire mesh which prevented the escape of fumes at temperatures high enough to ignite gases. The museum is open Monday to Friday, and Sunday afternoons, but is closed on bank holidays in winter. Tel: Manchester 736–1832.

Saltaire, West Yorkshire ☆   MAP B

Now a district of Shipley, on the north-west side of Bradford, the former model village or small town of Saltaire was the creation of Sir Titus Salt, who built there in 1853 a palatial six-storey wool mill of stone and cast iron. Around this factory, Salt built a complete new village to house his workers, away from the grime and smoke of Bradford where they were accustomed to living in cramped back-to-back houses with primitive sanitation and facilities. Sir Titus Salt's enterprise was one of the first positive responses to the questions asked by the rioting and suffering of the exploited workers of the Industrial Revolution. In the Yorkshire wool mills, the owners were often cruel task-masters. Children, as well as men and women, worked crippling hours for low wages, and lived in appalling conditions. Saltaire had a school, hospital, baths, laundry, church and, above all, fresh air, as the estate had its own park, described at the time as 'the most beautiful in the world'. The workers' cottages were in terraced rows and built on two storeys, with kitchen, parlour and two bedrooms. Foremen and managers had slightly better places to live in, naturally, and Salt, like all Victorian philanthropists, saw himself also as the guardian of his workers' morals – there was no pub. The village was soon made out of date by the more famous industrial estates of Bournville and Port Sunlight, but Salt was a

pioneer of decent housing for industrial workers, and the place still stands
as its founder's monument, little changed though now surrounded by
Bradford's less imaginative suburbs.

Saltash, Cornwall   =   MAP A

The Royal Albert Bridge across the River Tamar was built by Isambard
Kingdom Brunel (*q.v.*) between 1853 and 1859. The bridge is over two
thousand feet in length and was built to carry the so-called South Devon
Railway over the wide river estuary into Cornwall. The bridge is of
combined arch and suspension type, and is by no stretch of the imagination
a thing of beauty, but in engineering terms it was a triumph, and Brunel's
last and most spectacular contribution to the man-made landscape. Huge
crowds gathered to watch with bated breath as the central girders, each
weighing more than a thousand tons, were floated into position on
pontoons on the river during the rising tide, and came to rest within an
accuracy of an eighth of an inch. Although the bridge was named in honour
of the Prince Consort, who opened it in 1859, it carries proudly and
prominently the name of its creator, I.K. Brunel, who died later that year.

Saltburn, Cleveland   +   MAP B

The cliff railway here was built in 1884 to replace a vertical lift installed in
1869 when the Quaker ironmaster Henry Pease developed the town as a
seaside resort. The track has a gradient of 1 in 1.33, and the cars are
operated by water ballast.

Santon Downham, Norfolk   △   MAP A

North of the village of Santon Downham, in a large clearing in the pine
forest, is a landscape of craters and spoil-heaps made by men of the New
Stone Age in what was clearly a prehistoric boom industry. Christian
superstition had labelled the place Grime's Graves, identifying the Norse
god Odin or 'Grim' with the Devil, long before Canon Greenwell discovered in 1870 that this place had nothing to do with death or burial but was
a Neolithic tool factory. Four thousand years ago, men dug shafts through
the chalk rock to reach the layers of flint, which they mined and fashioned
into axes and other tools and weapons such as knives and arrow-heads, to
supply a demand throughout southern England and for export to the
Continent. The mine shafts were sometimes forty feet deep and occasionally had galleries or tunnels radiating from them. The tools the earliest

miners used to dig the flint – presumably only until they had made more efficient tools of flint for their own use – were picks made from deer antlers, and they worked in the dark mines by the light of tallow lamps, which left tell-tale sooty marks on the roofs of the galleries. There was a shrine at the site with chalk fertility figures, which can still be seen, and one of the mine shafts has been made accessible to the public. The site is open daily throughout the year except Sunday mornings.

Saxtead, Suffolk ×   MAP A

The fine 46-foot high windmill at Saxtead Green is an eighteenth-century post mill, restored to working order by the Department of the Environment as an Ancient Monument, and open to the public. The weatherboarded body or 'buck' of the mill stands above a two-storey brick base, and the sails drive two pairs of millstones.

Scafell Pike, Cumbria △   MAP B

On the south-west side of England's highest mountain, just below the summit, and on other Lake District fells such as the southern slopes of Pike of Stickle in Langdale, prehistoric factory sites have been found, where men of the Stone Age made stone axes and other primitive tools four thousand years ago. Archaeologists had discovered as far away as Dorset and South Wales axes and implements which could only have come from the Lake District, being made from volcanic tuff, which flakes like flint when struck and can be worked to a sharp edge. The Pike of Stickle site was discovered in 1947, and the Scafell one in 1959. Roughly shaped implements have been found at these sites, and it is assumed that these were made here and then transported by mountain tracks down to settlements near the coast where they were finished by shaping and polishing. The Scafell Pike factory can certainly lay indisputable claim to being the highest industrial site in England. The Lakeland fells can be dangerous places for the inexperienced, however, and should not be climbed without expert guidance. Products of these Neolithic axe factories can be seen in the museum at Carlisle and in the Museum of Lakeland Life and Industry at Kendal (*q.v.*).

Seaham, Durham ○   MAP B

A town and harbour were built here, commencing in 1828, for the shipment of coal from the third Marquess of Londonderry's mines.

Wooden 'chaldron' wagons (made to carry a measured weight of coal) ran
on wagonways right on to the wharves, or 'staithes', where the wagons were
lifted by coal drops and lowered to the decks of waiting ships, so that coal
could be unloaded into their holds without excessive breakage. A coal drop
was a swing lift in the form of a counterbalanced iron beam. Chauldron
wagons and the last surviving coal drop from Seaham can be seen at the
North of England Open Air Museum near Stanley (*q.v.*).

Seathwaite, Cumbria △   MAP B

A thousand feet up the fells above Seathwaite are mine adits and diminutive spoil-heaps of the 'wadd' mining industry, which had its heyday in the
eighteenth century at the same time, and with something like the same
excess of zeal, as the Klondike Gold Rush. The stuff dug out from beneath
the rocks of Borrowdale was not gold, and it did not glitter, but it was buried
treasure to the industrialists who rushed to exploit it. What the locals had
long called 'wadd' was actually graphite, also called 'black lead' or 'plumba-
go', and it turned out that here were the world's purest deposits of the stuff,
which the local farmers had used to brand their Herdwick sheep and their
wives ground to a paste and administered in white wine as a cure-all. But it
had a wide industrial application as a preservative against rust, a fixing
agent for dyes, a metal for casting shot, a glazing for pottery and was ideal
for black-leading fire grates and as pencil lead. There was much illicit
mining and smuggling of the stuff when the local folk realized they had
been sitting on a fortune, and an Act of Parliament of 1752 provided dire
penalties for theft – one of many precautions taken to protect the deposits.
One mine yielded £44,000 worth of graphite in 1778, and another more
than £100,000 in 1803. By this time most of the 'wadd' was going to the
pencil manufacturers in Keswick, and by the late 1830s the deposits were
practically exhausted.

Seaton, Devon +   MAP A

The bridge carrying the coast road over the mouth of the River Axe is
reputed to be Britain's oldest surviving concrete road bridge. Lines in the
surface of the material were intended to simulate masonry joints. The
bridge was built in 1877.

Seaton Sluice, Northumberland ○   MAP B

Seaton Sluice was one of the less successful building enterprises of the

Industrial Revolution. The Delaval coal-owners constructed an artificial harbour here in the 1760s for the export of their coal. It was necessary to cut through solid rock to make an eastern outlet, to replace their earlier and by now inadequate northern outlet. Their shipping berth was protected by sluice gates at the mouth of the channel, and a planned village was established which the Delavals visualized developing into a large town. But it was Blyth (*q.v.*) which grew at Seaton Sluice's expense, and after a century the dock ceased its working life. It remains as a haven for small boats, with houses on the island created by the two outlets.

Seil Island, Strathclyde +   MAP D

The Clachan Bridge linking the island with the mainland (B844) was designed by Telford (*q.v.*), and is whimsically said to be the only bridge to cross the Atlantic, though road bridges in the Orkney Isles and the Outer Hebrides have better claims to the title.

Selby, North Yorkshire +   MAP B

The timber toll bridge crossing the River Ouse at this inland port was built around 1790, and is believed to be the earliest such wooden bridge surviving in England.

Shalford, Surrey ×   MAP A

Shalford Mill on the River Tillingbourne is a restored eighteenth-century water mill in the care of the National Trust. The building is on three storeys, the ground floor being of brick and the upper floors tile-hung. The second floor has an overhang supported by wooden posts, and contains the hoist. The breastshot iron wheel, which drove three pairs of stones, remains intact. The mill is open daily.

Shap, Cumbria △   MAP B

South of the town, beside the A6, are the famous Shap granite quarries (not open) which still produce very hard stone for heavy constructional work, but also a pinkish variety, from a quarry opened in 1868, used as an ornamental building stone. This is a porphyritic granite with crystals of feldspar. It was only with the coming of the railway that it became a practical proposition to open up quarries at such remote sites, and the railways themselves have been among the quarries' chief customers, using Shap

granite for ballast. It is also widely used in road-making. The bollards
round London's St Paul's Cathedral are of Shap granite.

Shaw, Greater Manchester   ×   MAP B

Shaw was reputed at one time to be the richest of the cotton-spinning
towns of Lancashire, with millionaires a-plenty and the largest mills.
Limited liability companies were largely financed by the working men
themselves, who were apt to invade the place in huge numbers when new
shares were on offer. Among the multi-storey brick mills and chimney
stacks to be seen here is Dee Mill, where the Northern Mill Engine Society
preserves a horizontal twin-tandem compound steam engine built in 1906
to drive all the mill's machinery. It was built by Scott and Hodgson, and was
the most sophisticated of steam factory engines.

Sheerness, Kent   ○   MAP A

The Boatstore at Sheerness Docks is an iron-framed four-storey building
which one might easily mistake for a very modern piece of commercial
architecture. In fact it was built in 1859, and was designed by the Admiralty
architect Col. G.T. Greene. Iron beams and columns avoid load-bearing
walls, and this unlikely Victorian building is one of the earliest of its kind.
The naval dockyards at Chatham (*q.v.*) and Portsmouth were in the
vanguard of new building methods in the nineteenth century. The Royal
Navy relinquished Sheerness Dockyard in 1960.

Sheffield, South Yorkshire   □   MAP B

Cutlers' Hall, with its classical facade in Church Street, was built in 1832
and is both a symbol and headquarters of the city's pre-eminence in making
cutting tools – knives and axes, saws and sickles, shears and scissors.
Sheffield's fame for cutting tools goes back to medieval times, but its
modern industry owes much to a Doncaster clockmaker, Benjamin Hunts-
man, who invented the 'crucible' technique of making steel of high quality.
Stainless steel came into use in the present century with the addition of
nickel to the alloy, which increases its tensile strength and resists corrosion.
The Hall is the office of the Cutlers' Company which was established in
1624 to control the quality of all goods bearing the trade mark 'Sheffield
Steel'. Several other survivals tell the story of the city's industrial past. The
Balfour works in Broughton Lane are the largest remaining crucible steel
shops, while on the premises of the British Iron and Steel Research

Association in Hoyle Street is the country's only remaining complete cementation furnace, in which iron was roasted in charcoal furnaces to produce steel by the absorption of carbon. *See also* Abbeydale Industrial Hamlet.

Sheffield, South Yorkshire ✕ 　　　MAP B

In Endcliffe Park, Hangingwater Road, west of the city, is the so-called Shepherd Wheel, an iron overshot waterwheel of eighteen-foot diameter which drove the machinery of a nineteenth-century grinding workshop, restored and maintained with much original equipment by Sheffield City Museum. It is open to visitors Wednesday to Sunday throughout the year.

Sheldon, Derbyshire △ 　　　MAP B

South of the village is Magpie Mine, the most impressive of Peak lead-mining remains, all of which are in the care of the Peak District Mines Historical Society, which runs a museum of the industry at Matlock Bath. The lead industry of the Derbyshire Dome had existed since Roman times, and the miners had their own traditions and courts, which regulated the trade and judged upon their disputes. Defoe described the miners in the eighteenth century – men of 'a strange, turbulent, quarrelsome temper', who spent their lives of toil deep in the dark bowels of the earth, clad entirely in leather, for five pence a day. The industry expanded as the uses for lead increased – for plumbing and roofing and in the manufacture of paint and sulphuric acid among other things – but elaborate and costly drainage systems and pumping engines were necessary to keep the workings dry, and local mining became uneconomical when lead prices were forced down by foreign competition. The remains of Magpie Mine include an engine house and chimney, manual winding gear (called a 'stowse') and several subsidiary buildings, as well as mine shafts. Thousands of dangerous old shafts are dotted about the Peak District, most of them uncovered and unprotected, and visitors should always seek expert guidance in exploring the remains of the lead-mining industry.

Shipham, Somerset △ 　　　MAP A

In a field near the village church is the chimney of a former calamine calcining plant. Calcination is the process of refining ore by burning away the impurities. Calamine is a zinc ore, closely associated, industrially, with lead mining, and it was used locally in brass foundries as well as in the well known lotion.

Shorwell, Isle of Wight   ✕   MAP A

At Yafford, three-quarters of a mile south-west of the village, is a fully restored watermill, Yafford Mill, built in the eighteenth century. The millpond turns an overshot waterwheel, driving the two pairs of millstones which ground flour for the local population. Much restored agricultural machinery can also be seen here by visitors between April and October. Tel: Brighstone 740610.

Shotley Bridge, Durham   ☐   MAP B

The Derwent valley area has a curious tradition of sword-making, and in the late seventeenth century sword-cutlers came here from Solingen, the German equivalent of Sheffield, fleeing from religious persecution there. In Wood Street one or two of the cottages built for them remain, one having a poetic inscription in German on it. About a century afterwards, one of the families had become prosperous enough to build a large house at Bonfield-side, which is still known as Cutler's Hall.

Shrewsbury, Shropshire   ☆   MAP B

The problem of fire was a major one in early mills and factories – particularly in multi-storey buildings with timber floors and beams. The earliest practical answer to the problem was found by Charles Bage, who built a flax spinning mill here in 1796 which had a frame of iron. The four-storey brick building had cast-iron columns, beams and window frames, and an iron-framed roof. The building happily survives, north of the town centre at Ditherington, and is still in use, though now as maltings.

Shugborough, Staffordshire   =   MAP B

When the Earl of Lichfield permitted the Trent Valley Railway line between Rugeley and Stafford to cross the southern part of Shugborough Park in 1847, it was necessary to construct a bridge and a tunnel, and the architect John Livock took care to provide cosmetic treatment in keeping with the stately home's other notable ornamental architecture. One of the tunnel's entrances has a mock-medieval portal with battlements, and that at the other end is in Egyptian style.

Singleton, West Sussex ☆   MAP A

The Weald and Downland Open Air Museum at this village a few miles
north of Chichester has, among its other interesting exhibits, various old
timber buildings removed from their original sites and re-erected for
preservation here. There are also illustrations of the local iron industry,
which was very important here until the Industrial Revolution brought
mass production and gave other areas the technical advantage. The Weald
is an area between the North and South Downs where the rock yielded ore
and made the region the principal centre of iron working in Britain until the
eighteenth century. Armaments were the chief products of many of the
works in their latter days. The last furnace to work in the south-east was at
Ninfield, which was operative until 1820. There are few remains of the
hundred or more former sites of iron working, except the so-called
'hammer ponds' whose water supplied power for the forges. These can still
be seen, especially in St Leonard's Forest between Horsham and Crawley.
The museum is open every day from January to October. Tel: Liphook
723104.

Sissinghurst, Kent ▲   MAP A

At Sissinghurst Castle, on the A262 north east of Cranbrook, and best
known for its fine gardens laid out by Vita Sackville-West, there is a good
group of preserved oast houses, the main part of which has been converted
into a tea-room. Most of Kent's traditional oast houses, with their familiar
white cowls, have now been bought up as private homes as the old method
of drying hops has become out of date. Most were built in the nineteenth
century, and were designed to retain heat. The harvested hops were spread
on a drying floor halfway up the kiln, and hot air was blown up through
them and let out at the top. The air temperature could be controlled by trap
doors beneath the cowls, for it is important not to overheat the hops,
otherwise the oils essential to the brewing process would evaporate. Kent
grows over half the hops used by British breweries – one of the best areas to
see them growing is in the valley of the River Medway and its tributaries to
the east of Tonbridge.

Skipton, North Yorkshire ✕   MAP B

The Leatt Industrial and Folk Museum at High Mill on Chapel Hill is a
restored and working corn mill driven by the water of the Eller Beck, with
two wheels, one of which has a diameter of 28 feet. The mill belonged to

the Skipton Castle estate once, but is now a private museum open on
Sunday and bank holiday afternoons.

Slaggyford, Northumberland   =   MAP B

Farther south along the line from Lambley (*q.v.*) on the Alston branch of
the Newcastle and Carlisle Railway, is the remarkable stone viaduct, also
built in 1852, which is not half as large, but is arguably twice as interesting.
It crosses the Thinhope Burn and the main road, and is of skew-arch
construction, but it has more arches on one side than on the other. Because
of the angles involved, there are six arches on the west side and five on the
other, the longer side having a blind arch to make up the length.

Sleaford, Lincolnshire   ▲   MAP B

The former Bass Maltings, on the town's southern outskirts, are an
example of industrial building on the grand scale. They are nearly 1,000
feet in length – twice as long as Lincoln Cathedral – and were completed in
1905. They are of brick on 6 storeys, forming 8 detached pavilions, with a
square 4-storey engine house in the middle and a water tower above it.
Each pavilion has a projecting timber-framed crane hood. The engine
house was built for 2 horizontal tandem compound engines which could
pump water at the rate of 27,000 gallons a minute from an artesian well
bored in 1892. The buildings are still in commercial use, though now by
separate companies and not as maltings.

Smethwick, West Midlands   ×   MAP A

The Soho Foundry, in Foundry Street east of the town centre, is the home
of Avery scales and weighing machines, and the company maintains a
private museum which interested visitors can see by prior arrangement.
The premises are more interesting, however (with all due respect to Messrs
Avery), as the site where Matthew Boulton and James Watt (*q.v.*) carried
out their great work on improving the steam engine. The two men formed
their famous partnership in 1775 and, twenty years later, built a new factory
here devoted entirely to making their steam engines. Little remains of their
buildings, but the modern factory stands on an historic site in industrial
terms. Tel: Birmingham 558 1112.

Smethwick, West Midlands ≈   MAP A

The extraordinary Engine Arm Aqueduct, carrying a branch of the
Birmingham Canal over the main cutting, was built by Telford (*q.v.*) in
1828. Telford's mastery of cast iron was never more clearly shown than in
this positively medieval piece of design, with 22 gothic arches forming a
decorative tracery above the single broad arch between masonry abutments.

Smitham Hill, Somerset △   MAP A

A little to the south-west of the village of East Harptree is the chimney stack
of the former local lead works. Built in the mid-nineteenth century, the
stack is very much like those of the tin mines so familiar to us in Cornwall,
with a stone base and brick top. All the remaining buildings of this works
were demolished when the company went bust, but the chimney was left
and has been restored.

Snailbeach, Shropshire △   MAP B

Several remains of lead mines can be seen in the vicinity of this village on
the western side of the range of hills known as the Stiperstones. The mines
were worked during the Roman occupation, when the imperial forces
extracted silver for their coinage and zinc from these hills as well. Pigs of
lead bearing Hadrian's name have been found, and lead continued to be
extracted intermittently until, during the Industrial Revolution, it was
mined on a more ambitious scale from what was then one of the richest
seams in England. The bleak and desolate nature of the area is well
reflected in the place names – Squilver, The Bog, Black Marsh, etc.
Boulton and Watt pumping engines were installed in the mines and
development of the site continued until the last quarter of the nineteenth
century. A chapel called the Lord's Chapel was built at Snailbeach for the
mining community, and by-products such as arsenic were exploited and a
railway constructed to serve the industry. The mines were practically
exhausted by early in this century, however, and the majority of miners
departed, leaving behind them a weird landscape of derelict engine houses
like the ruined keeps of tiny castles, with dangerous open shafts and pits
and white spoil-heaps defiling the scene; whilst the remaining scattered
population had to adapt to making its living from agriculture.

Lead mines at Snailbeach

Snape, Suffolk ▲   MAP A

On the south bank of the River Alde, south of the village, are the Snape Maltings, now world-famous. Part of this large nineteenth-century complex is still in commercial use, but another part, badly damaged by fire in 1969, has been rebuilt as a concert hall and is used by the Aldeburgh Festival created by Benjamin Britten. The maltings are of brick and weatherboarding with hoists for barley on the old quayside.

Soham, Cambridgeshire   +   MAP A

In the period of the turnpike roads, a levy was imposed by an Act of 1741 on loads over a certain limit, and led to the appearance of the 'steelyard' – a large weighing machine projecting from the wall of a building, on which wagons of hay and such-like loads were weighed by means of a long cantilevered beam. The steelyard at Soham, near the Fountain Hotel, is one of the only two remaining large steelyards in Britain.

South Queensferry, Lothian   =   MAP D

Thomas Bouch, builder of the first Tay railway bridge (*see* Dundee) had
already begun construction of a suspension bridge across the Forth when
the Tay disaster occurred. Not surprisingly, the Forth project came to a
sudden halt. New engineers were appointed – John Fowler and Benjamin
Baker – and they built a steel cantilever bridge, supported by towers built
on caissons sunk into the river bed. It cost 3 million pounds and the lives of
57 men, and took 8 years to complete. It carries a double track 150 feet
above water level via two main spans each nearly ⅓ mile in length. The
bridge's total length is 1½ miles. It was opened in 1890 and was at the time
the world's longest cantilever bridge.

South Shields, Tyne & Wear   ○   MAP B

The nineteenth-century scene here is well depicted by Turner's famous
painting of 1835, now in the National Gallery of Art in Washington D.C.,
of 'Keelmen heaving in Coals by Night'. Dozens of sailing ships were lined
up along the wharves, where the light of dockside fires contrasted with the
pale moonlight, both filtering through a smoky haze. When Turner painted
the scene the railway was in embryo. Most of the older buildings and
machinery have been replaced, where docks now stretch along three miles
of the Tyne estuary. But this is also where the world's first self-righting
lifeboat was invented, and where the first lifeboat service began. A model of
the lifeboat is in the town's museum, and a monument to its inventor,
William Wouldhave, stands in Ocean Road.

Springwell, Tyne & Wear   =   MAP B

The Bowes Railway, now preserved by a trust, was originally a mineral line
designed by George Stephenson (*q.v.*) in 1826. It operated at one time both
with locomotives and stationary steam engines, as well as a gravity incline,
and ran from the coal mines at Mount Moor to the port at Jarrow.
Workshops, locomotives and rolling stock can be seen here.

Standedge, West Yorkshire   ≈   MAP B

The Standedge Tunnel, on the Huddersfield Narrow Canal, is the longest
canal tunnel ever built in this country. Nearly 3¼ miles long, it was cut
through the solid rock of the Pennines and completed in 1811. The canal
itself is only 7½ feet wide in parts, but wider caverns were blasted out of the

rock every so often as passing places for the boats, which took more than 3 hours to negotiate the tunnel. Despite all the effort and engineering works on this canal, which had 74 locks on its 20-mile course, it was never a great commercial success, and although not finally abandoned until 1944, little commercial traffic used it after the turn of the century.

Stanhill, Lancashire ☆   MAP B

The Post Office of this village near Oswaldtwistle is the house in which James Hargreaves lived, and where he invented the 'Spinning Jenny'. He was a hand-loom weaver by trade and a carpenter by inclination, and it was in 1764 that he invented and built his 'Jenny', the principle of which was that a spinning wheel could operate a *series* of spindles, not just one. Local spinners saw this gadget as a threat to their livelihoods, and several of Hargreaves's new machines were smashed when a mob attacked his home here. Hargreaves, like Arkwright (*q.v.*) afterwards, went to the Midlands, where new ideas were better received, and he died in Nottingham.

Stanley, Durham ☆   MAP B

A mile and a half north-east of Stanley beside the road to Chester le Street
is Beamish Hall, a nineteenth-century stone-built mansion, in the grounds
of which is the North of England Open Air Museum, one of the best of its
kind in the country. It is a major source of interest and information on the
industry of north-east England, with particularly comprehensive exhibits
on coal-mining. The site was acquired from the National Coal Board by
the county council. There is an accessible drift mine (which one enters on
foot down an adit instead of descending a shaft); an example of the vertical
winding gear peculiar to this part of the country; and rebuilt pitmen's
cottages. There is also the only surviving coal drop, brought here from
Seaham (*q.v.*). As well as coal mining there are sections on transport, with
preserved steam locomotives; and agricultural tools and machinery. Open
every day except winter Mondays. Tel: Stanley 231811.

Stanley, West Yorkshire ≈   MAP B

At this location north-east of Wakefield is the remarkable Stanley Ferry
Aqueduct, which carries the Aire and Calder Canal over the River Calder.
It was built in 1839 and consists of an iron trough suspended from an arch
of cast iron spanning the river.

Stanton Drew, Avon +   MAP A

A former toll-house survives on the B3130 north of the village, built on two
storeys and hexagonal in shape, with a thatched roof.

Stapleford, Nottinghamshire ☐   MAP B

In Nottingham Road there is a group of early nineteenth-century brick
cottages of the sort familiar in the Midland textile counties, with long rows
of windows on the top floors where, in this case, lace-makers had their
workshops before the rise of factory industry.

GEORGE AND ROBERT STEPHENSON

The Stephensons, father and son, were born at Wylam and Newcastle-on-
Tyne (*q.v.*) respectively, in 1781 and 1803. George became a mining
engineer, and among other things invented a safety lamp at the same time
as Sir Humphry Davy. His early experiments with locomotives were for

NOTICE

Opposite
*Winding engine
at Beamish
Museum,
Stanley* colliery transport. He became the engineer of the Stockton and Darlington Railway in 1822, and subsequently of the Liverpool and Manchester Railway, when his engine 'Rocket' made its successful trial run at Rainhill (*q.v.*). The triumph of this demonstration that a steam engine could successfully and reliably haul trains was the beginning of the great railway revolution, and the basic principles on which Stephenson built his locomotives remained virtually unaltered throughout the 130 – or so – years of steam locomotive engineering. George's son Robert assisted in building 'Rocket'. He only outlived his father, who died in 1848, by 11 years, but likewise became an outstanding railway engineer and architect and M.P. for Whitby. His greatest work was the construction of the London and Birmingham Railway, but he also built some notable bridges (including the pioneering Britannia tubular bridge across the Menai Strait – lost through fire in 1970). He was himself a mine-owner. His company designed railways and built locomotives for many other countries as well as Britain. The Stephensons established, among other things, the standard gauge of 4 feet 8½ inches, which is thought to have been adopted from the usual width between horse-drawn tram wheels in use at the time.

Stevington, Bedfordshire ✕   MAP A

The restored windmill here was built around 1770–80, and is a timber post mill above a round brick lower storey. The original sails (now replaced) drove the millstones, used for grinding corn, which are still *in situ*. The mill is open to the public daily.

Stewartby, Bedfordshire ☆   MAP A

The clay land of the London Basin and the northern Home Counties, with their dearth of suitable stone for building, was the natural location for large brickworks, particularly after the Great Fire of London gave a tremendous impetus to building in brick instead of timber. In the 1920s Sir Malcolm Stewart began this model village for his workers, with shops, school and all mod cons, after he had taken over the small local brick factory. The mass production of bricks exploits what geologists call the Oxford Clay, which has a high carbon content and so is economical in firing. Expansion of the local industry was very rapid, and Stewartby is now the home of the largest brick works in the world, the London Brick Company, whose forests of tall chimneys belch smoke from furnaces capable of firing around 850 million bricks a year.

Opposite
Post mill at
Avoncroft
Museum,
Stoke Prior

Sticklepath, Devon □   MAP A

A rural museum of industry has been set up in what was formerly the iron
'foundry' of Finch Brothers, who made agricultural edge tools and equipment for the china clay industry. The buildings date from the eighteenth
century, having been built originally as corn and cloth mills. The works
were powered by three waterwheels driven by the River Taw, one of them
operating a pair of tilt-hammers which remain *in situ*.

Stockton-on-Tees, Cleveland =   MAP B

South of the town centre, in Bridge Street, is the former booking office of
the Stockton and Darlington Railway. It is a tiny brick cottage – No. 48 (not
open).

Stoke Bruerne, Northamptonshire ≈   MAP A

The Waterways Museum, on the Grand Union Canal near Blisworth
tunnel (*q.v.*) is housed in a stone-built three-storey former grain warehouse. Open-air exhibits include a boat-weighing machine and a restored
narrow boat, while inside there is a reconstruction of a typical 'butty' cabin
with traditional decoration and displays showing the history and relics of
the canal industry and the life of the boat people. The museum is open daily
except winter Mondays and at Christmas. Tel: Northampton 862229.

Stoke-on-Trent, Staffordshire □   MAP B

Stoke-on-Trent was created as a County Borough in 1910 from six former
towns known the world over as the Potteries. They were Burslem, Fenton,
Hanley, Longton, Stoke and Tunstall (*qq.v.*), and the names survive as
areas of the city which is now one of a baker's dozen of the largest in
England. No one knows when pottery first began to be made here, but the
area was certainly known for it in the fourteenth century, and finds of
Roman and Saxon pottery suggest that the local tradition is very ancient.
The explanation lies in the availability of suitable clay and water supplies
and – as far as the great expansion in the Industrial Revolution is concerned
– coal supplies as well. 'Pottery' is a term embracing several different kinds
of product, including earthenware, stoneware, bone china and porcelain,
each having its own special ingredients, techniques and characteristics.
The aristocrat of them all is porcelain, for long a secret of the Chinese, and
only discovered by European manufacturers in the early eighteenth cen-

Opposite
*Maharajah's
Well at Stoke
Row*
tury. The secret was the chief ingredient, kaolin (china clay), and if it had not been for the long Staffordshire tradition and ideal placing for other raw materials and fuel, the English potteries might well have been established in Cornwall (*see* Carthew). As it was, leading potters such as Josiah Wedgwood (*q.v.*), Thomas Minton, William Copeland and Job Ridgeway spent time in the south-west working out trading deals with the owners of the china clay works. But English manufacturers modified the classic process of porcelain-making by using the ash of burned animal bones as their 'flux' (which assists fusion of the other ingredients) and called the resulting ware 'bone china', which was universally adopted in Britain and has remained virtually exclusive to this country. The individual sites and remains of the earlier potteries are given under the names of the former towns mentioned above, but for reasons of space they are all identified on the map as Stoke-on-Trent. In Stoke itself (London Road) is Minton's modern factory, with a fine museum of the company's products; and the parish church has monuments to Wedgwood and Josiah Spode, among others, while a statue of Josiah Wedgwood stands, contemplating one of his own pots, outside the railway station.

Stoke Prior, Hereford & Worcester ☆ MAP A

The Avoncroft Museum of Buildings is at this village near Bromsgrove. It is an open-air collection of mainly industrial and agricultural buildings which have been rescued from demolition and re-erected here. They include nailers' and chainmakers' workshops, and a fine fully operational windmill with a brick base and timber superstructure; all its working parts can be seen. Open daily from March to November. Tel: Bromsgrove 31363.

Stoke Row, Oxfordshire ☆ MAP A

Among the village's council houses is a little garden with a slightly bizarre reminder of the difficulties experienced in the chalky Chilterns in obtaining drinking water before piped supplies were introduced. The Governor of India's North-West Provinces in the days of the Raj was Edward Reade of nearby Ipsden, and he told the Maharajah of Benares about Stoke Row's water problems. The Maharajah undertook to remedy the situation, and generously paid for a well to be dug. It was completed in 1864 and is 368 feet deep. It is surmounted by an oriental cupola with a model of an Indian elephant above the winding gear.

Stonehaven, Grampian ☆   MAP D

In the market square is a house with a plaque marking the site of Robert Thomson's birthplace in 1822. Thomson was the inventor of, among other things, dry docks, various steam engines, and the pneumatic tyre, which he invented in 1845 and fitted to horse-drawn carriages, but which did not catch on for forty years.

Stornoway, Lewis ☐   MAP D

The weaving of Harris tweed has remained a cottage industry in the Hebrides since the seventeenth century, when owning clans such as the Seaforth Mackenzies allowed their crofter tenants to farm the land and engage in cottage manufacturing. The wool is spun and dyed in mills at Stornoway, the 'capital' of Lewis (of which Harris is the southern part), but is still woven on hand looms by the crofters, who sometimes pile the woven tweed up at the roadside to await collection by the mills. Several places on this island are open to visitors who wish to see the weaving of Harris tweed in progress, and there are crofters' cottages preserved as museums.

Stourbridge, West Midlands ☐   MAP A

The Stuart Crystal works, off the A491 north-west of the town centre, preserves a glass cone dating from around 1780, one of only a handful remaining in Britain, although at one time every large town would have possessed its own glass works. This cone is built of brick and is nearly ninety feet tall, and was originally called Redhouse Glassworks. Although a glass cone looks similar from the outside to a 'bottle' kiln in the Potteries, it was actually quite different. Whereas a pottery kiln was just an oven for firing the products, the glass cone was an entire factory, with a working area round a central furnace. Arched entrances at ground level admitted men and materials. Pots of glass were heated in the furnace, and finished products were cooled very slowly in annealing hearths in the walls of the cone, in order to prevent cracking by too sudden changes of temperature. Visitors can see round the works by prior arrangement. Tel: Brierley Hill 71161.

Stowmarket, Suffolk   MAP A

The Abbot's Hall Museum is an open-air agricultural museum with buildings and implements which include a water mill and a medieval farmhouse which have been re-erected on the site, and a sixteenth-century barn which was built here. There is a collection of ploughs and farm wagons. Although East Anglia was generally backward in adopting mechanical aids in farming, it produced pioneers such as Jethro Tull and 'Turnip' Townshend, and many inventions came from the region, Ransomes of Ipswich being in the forefront of developing advanced ploughs made of cast iron. The museum is open daily during the summer months except Sunday mornings. Tel: Stowmarket 612229.

Stratford-on-Avon, Warwickshire ≈ MAP A

The Stratford Canal was opened in 1816 – having been commenced nearly twenty years earlier – to link the Avon with the Worcester and Birmingham Canal. The various hold-ups in progress were due to lack of finance. The first engineer was Josiah Clowes, who died within three years; the second his former assistant Samuel Porter; and the third William James. The canal's terminus is a basin beside the Royal Shakespeare Theatre. Among its most interesting features are the foot-bridges of cast iron which have narrow gaps through the deck and parapets so that horses' tow ropes could pass through without being disconnected from the barges. This end of the restored canal is owned by the National Trust.

Street, Somerset □ MAP A

The well known shoe manufacturers C. and J. Clark have been established in Street since 1825, and part of their original factory of 1829 has been converted into a museum of shoes and leathercraft, including displays of footwear going back to the Roman occupation. The museum is open on weekdays in the summer months. Tel: Street 43131.

Stretham, Cambridgeshire ✕ MAP A

The pumping station here contains a Boulton and Watt beam engine built in 1831 and preserved by the Stretton Engine Preservation Trust. It was installed to drive a waterwheel, ironically reversing the whole point of earlier waterwheels. Instead of the waterwheel driving the machinery, the machinery here drove the wheel, which scooped up water from the fenland to a drainage channel. A larger wheel, still *in situ*, which could raise water at a rate of more than 100 tons a minute, was installed in 1896. It has a diameter of 37 feet, and took over the work of many windmills in the area. The station can be seen by visitors.

Sturminster Marshall, Dorset   ✕   MAP A

By the River Stour north-east of the village are the remains of White Mill, an eighteenth-century corn mill powered by two waterwheels which drove its wooden machinery.

Styal, Cheshire   ☆   MAP B

Quarry Bank Mill, built in 1784, is the nucleus of the best preserved factory colony of the Industrial Revolution. Samuel Greg, one of the pioneers of the factory system, built this textile mill of brick in the valley of the River Bollin, and around it developed his model village. There are rows of workers' cottages, manager's house, apprentices' house, chapel, school and shop, all built by Greg in a setting which, like Saltaire (*q.v.*) half a century later, was chosen to provide a more attractive and healthy industrial community than was possible in the overcrowded and insanitary towns and cities. The whole colony is preserved by the National Trust. The mill itself is a working museum of the cotton industry and the apprentices' house has exhibits on the social history of the village. Open to visitors on afternoons of most days except Mondays throughout the year, but only at weekends in the winter months. Tel: Wilmslow 527468.

Sunderland, Tyne & Wear   ○   MAP B

Illustrious names are connected with efforts to bridge the Wear at Sunderland, which had grown from its industrial origins as a shipbuilding centre in the fourteenth century. Tom Paine, author of *The Rights of Man*, was involved in an abortive attempt to put an iron bridge across the river in 1793, and Robert Stephenson (*q.v.*) built a bridge in 1858 replacing an earlier one. This has since been in turn replaced. Nineteenth-century warehouses and other buildings remain at the docks, and the North Pier, constructed to protect the harbour at the river's mouth, was originally built in 1787 and lengthened in 1841.

Sutton, Norfolk   ✕   MAP A

The nine-storey windmill is the tallest in Britain at just under 80 feet. This tower mill was originally built in 1798, but suffered fire damage and was rebuilt in 1857. Its patent sails drove four pairs of millstones. The mill is on a minor road east of the village, and has been restored.

Swanage, Dorset △   MAP A

Tilly Whim Caves, south of the town near Durlston Head, are actually the remains of adits from which Purbeck limestone was mined at one time. The local 'freestone' (stone which can be carved intricately because of its fine grain) was more popular in the Middle Ages than that from Portland (*q.v.*). It had been used by the Romans, who carted it as far as their town of Viroconium (Wroxeter) in Shropshire, and it appears in many of our cathedrals, where it is often called Purbeck Marble, because it is capable of taking a polished surface. Many quarries are still worked on the so-called Isle of Purbeck, and the Ancient Order of Marblers and Stonecutters meets annually in the town hall at Corfe, below the famous castle, which was built of the local stone in medieval times.

Swanage, Dorset ☆   MAP A

The Victorian water tower in Taunton Road is not the only bizarre building of the period in this seaside resort. It was built in 1886 in a style resembling the keep of a medieval castle, as if there were something indecent in visible evidence of a public water supply.

Swansea, West Glamorgan ☆   MAP C

The Maritime and Industrial Museum is located in the former South Dock, and deals with the history of the port, where Defoe remarked in the eighteenth century that 'one sometimes sees a hundred sail of ships at a time loading coals here'. The museum is open on weekdays throughout the year. Tel: Swansea 55006 or 50351.

Sway, Hampshire ☆   MAP A

Whether a folly can be encompassed by the definition of industry as 'useful labour' is a nice point, but I include Peterson's Tower, south of the village, as an example of several such fairly useless works undertaken around the country by benevolent landowners in order to provide work for the unemployed. This 218-foot tower was built by Andrew Peterson, who had been a judge in India, and its style was derived from Indian models. A half-excuse for including it here is that it was one of the early structures in concrete, having been built around 1885, when the material was still largely experimental, and Judge Peterson pioneered the 'shutter' method of building with it, setting the concrete in wooden frames and raising the building a few feet at a time. The tower is not accessible.

Swindon, Wiltshire   =   MAP A

Swindon was chosen as the site for the Great Western Railway's workshops
on the recommendation of Daniel Gooch, the company's chief locomotive
engineer. The town would be a convenient place to change engines for the
steeper gradients at the western end of the line, and a suitable point for the
junction with the proposed Gloucester and Cheltenham branch line. The
works were built of stone excavated from the tunnel at Box (*q.v.*) and
opened in 1843. Ten years later a housing estate had appeared for the
railway workers, and Swindon was rapidly being converted from what
Cobbett had called 'a plain country town' in 1821, with a population of
2,000, to a great railway metropolis and easily the biggest town in Wiltshire,
with over 12,000 men employed by the railway company alone in the early
years of the present century. The estate was planned by Sir Matthew Digby
Wyatt, who designed the station at Paddington (*q.v.*), and the streets were
named after towns on the G.W.R. route – Bristol Street, Taunton Street,
etc. The nucleus of the new town presents a fascinating piece of social/
industrial history. It had its own church, school, hospital and Mechanics'
Institute, all built by the railway company by the 1850s. In the following
decade, the estate was extended by the addition of Cambria Place, built for
Welsh workers, complete with Baptist chapel. By this time, speculators had
moved in on local housing expansion, and the railway company no longer
involved itself in housing. There was already a lodging house for Irish
workers in Faringdon Road, but this subsequently became a Methodist
chapel and is now the Railway Museum of the G.W.R., where some
historic locomotives are preserved. Open daily. Tel: Swindon 27211.

Swinton, South Yorkshire   □   MAP B

The famous Rockingham pottery works were established here in 1745, and
remained in operation for almost a century, making china similar to that of
the Derby and Coalport (*q.v.*) factories towards the end of its existence. A
ruined bottle oven survives at the site, west of the town centre.

Swithland, Leicestershire   △   MAP A

In Swithland Wood, near this village to the north-west of Leicester, are
several rain-filled pits which used to be quarries for the locally famous
Swithland slate, first worked by the Romans. From medieval times until the
nineteenth century, the slate was extracted for roofing purposes and for
millstones, kitchen sinks, cheese presses and, perhaps most interestingly,

gravestones. The hard laminated slate was found to be eminently suitable for engraving, and it weathered better than limestone or sandstone, which soon became illegible. Not only that, but it was lighter in weight, and thus easier and cheaper to transport, so it was used extensively in Leicestershire and neighbouring counties. The quarrymen were paid half-a-crown a day (12½ p in today's money) for drilling and blasting blocks of slate that might weigh over a ton, and they were raised from the bottoms of these pits by tackle and horse wheel. For roofing, it was much more attractive than the Welsh slate which eventually supplanted it, as it had variable colours – blue-grey, greenish and purple – which gleamed beautifully after rain and attracted lichens too. Roofs of Swithland slate can still be seen in the Charnwood Forest villages. The engraving of Swithland slate headstones became a distinctive local art form in the eighteenth and nineteenth centuries, when schoolmasters, parish clerks and other literate but poorly paid people with a talent for lettering earned a little extra in their spare time by this means. Usually, the calligraphic inscriptions and decorative motifs were incised in the slate, but the more ambitious and skilful craftsmen would sometimes painstakingly reduce the surface of the slate to leave their designs in relief, and towards the end over-flamboyant decoration degraded the style of the earlier work. Headstones of Swithland slate can be seen in most Leicestershire village churchyards, and in quantity at Loughborough, Narborough, and the churchyards of St Mary de Castro and St Margaret in Leicester.

 Tadcaster, North Yorkshire ▲   MAP B

Tadcaster has a long tradition of brewing, and John Smith's, west of the town centre, is the most spectacular of the town's breweries, with its ornate chimney and various architectural ornaments. The date 1883 is proclaimed above the main block with a huge magnet trade mark.

Tal-y-llyn, Gwynedd   =   MAP C

The village and its lake below Cader Idris gave their name to the now-famous narrow-gauge railway built in 1865 to serve the slate quarries, and still operated by a preservation society, running trains for the tourists in the summer months between Tywn (*q.v.*) and Abergynolwyn. The local quarries were closed soon after the Second World War, but the preservation society stepped in soon afterwards and prevented the railway from closing, giving the line a record for continuous service. Its gauge is 2 feet 3 inches.

Causey Arch at Tanfield

Tanfield, Durham   =   MAP B

The so-called Causey Arch is a stone-built bridge erected in 1727, and one
of the monuments to the history of railway development. It was built by a
stonemason, Ralph Wood, at a cost of over £2,000, to carry horse-drawn
wagons on rails, in order to convey coal from local collieries across the
valley of the stream to the main transport routes to Newcastle. The
structure is about 60 feet high and its arch has a span of 105 feet. It is
regarded as the oldest surviving railway bridge, and is one of the largest
masonry bridges built in Britain to carry a railway. It excited the wonder
and admiration of those who saw it for many years after its completion. The
bridge crosses the Tanfield Beck off the A6076 east of the village, and now
carries a footpath.

Tardebigge, Hereford & Worcester   ≈   MAP A

The flight of 30 narrow locks on the Worcester and Birmingham Canal is the longest in Britain. They were opened in 1815 and raise the level of the canal by 217 feet in the course of 2 miles. The summit lock is the deepest in the country at 14 feet. The canal itself has 58 locks and five tunnels along its 30 mile length linking Birmingham with the Severn at Worcester.

THOMAS TELFORD

The son of a Scottish shepherd, Telford was born in 1757, and when he was fourteen became a stonemason's apprentice. He was an accomplished craftsman by the time he went to London to further his ambition, and eventually he set up as an architect and building contractor. At the age of thirty he was appointed Surveyor of Public Works for the County of Salop. His years in Shropshire made his name as a civil engineer of outstanding talents. He built 40 road bridges in 5 years in that county alone, and then moved on to canal works, building the Ellesmere and Caledonian canals between 1796 and 1823, during which time he also built more than 1,000 miles of new roads and 1,200 bridges in Scotland. The poet Robert Southey dubbed him 'The Colossus of Roads'. The improvement of the London-Holyhead road, which included the building of the Menai suspension bridge (*q.v.*) was undoubtedly his greatest achievement. He also carried out important work on harbours, and built St Katharine Dock (*q.v.*) in London. He was the first President of the Institution of Civil Engineers, which he helped to found. He died in 1834, and was buried in Westminster Abbey.

Thaxted, Essex ×   MAP A

A brick-built four-storey tower mill of 1804 has been restored to working order here, and rivals the parish church as a local landmark. Three pairs of millstones used for grinding corn were driven by the sails. The mill stands beside the A130 north of the town centre.

Theale, Berkshire ≈   MAP A

A mile south of the village is Sheffield Lock on the Kennet Navigation. It is one of a series of 21 locks which raised boats 134 feet when the 18 miles of canal and navigable river were opened in 1723. The Sheffield Lock shows the early type of construction in which the lock walls were made of wood and turf, not brick or stone which came into use later.

Thornton Cleveleys, Lancashire ✕   MAP B

The windmill here is a little older than the one at Lytham St Annes (*q.v.*), having been built in 1794. It is of similar style, though taller (five storeys) – a white tower mill with its cap, like the one at Lytham, in the shape of an inverted boat. This former corn mill is called Marsh Mill and has been preserved by the local council.

Tiverton, Devon □   MAP A

On the night of June 28th, 1816, Luddite rebels broke into the lace factory of Heathcoat, Lacy and Boden at Loughborough, Leicestershire, and smashed 53 machines, worth £6,000, and shot and wounded a night watchman. Six men were hanged for this crime and John Heathcoat, who was the inventor of various technical improvements to the bobbin-net machines with which machine-lace was made, closed his factory down there. Leicestershire's loss was Devon's gain, for Mr Heathcoat came to Tiverton and set up business in an empty cotton mill, bringing many of his loyal workers with him. He built housing for them here in a distinctive Midland style. One of the new streets was even called Loughborough. Thus there was a revival of lace-making in what had been the most important industrial town in Devon because of its textile manufacturing. The modern factory on the site houses one of Europe's largest manufacturers of stretch fabrics, but the original gate lodges remain, and the planned terraces of workers' cottages all around, in Melbourne Street, Leat Street, St Paul's Street, etc., are worth looking at, as well as the school house built by Heathcoat in 1841 near the factory.

Torksey, Lincolnshire ≈   MAP B

At Torksey Lock, south of the village, the River Trent is joined by the oldest navigable canal in Britain. The Foss Dyke was cut by the Romans to link the River Trent with the Witham at Lincoln (*q.v.*), thus enabling barges to travel inland to military depots, carrying essential supplies to the imperial troops. The canal was planned by Roman engineers but no doubt dug by native labour. It was improved in the eighteenth century, but is still basically the canal made by the Romans nearly two thousand years ago.

Trefriw, Gwynedd □   MAP C

The Woollen Mill at this village on the River Crafnant dates from around

1830, and was powered by waterwheels until electricity was installed at the turn of the century. It specializes in the weaving of quilts, blankets and tweeds, and visitors can see all the processes from carding and spinning of the wool to the finished products. The mill is open to the public during normal working hours.

RICHARD TREVITHICK

Trevithick was born in 1771 at Camborne (*q.v.*) in Cornwall. His father was the manager of a mine and a friend of John Wesley. Richard went to school – intermittently – at Camborne, frequently played truant, and excelled only at weight-lifting and wrestling. But by the time he was in his mid-twenties he was building engines for the local tin mines and experimenting with model locomotives. The problem of pumping water out of the deep mine shafts was one of the major obstacles in the mining of tin, and Trevithick showed himself an engineer of genius in the design of efficient pumping engines, advancing the machines of Newcomen and Watt (*qq.v.*) with the invention of the 'Cornish' beam engine, soon installed in mines with names such as Ding Dong, Cook's Kitchen, etc., and subsequently all over the world. Trevithick's experiments with steam at high pressure led to his building the first steam railway locomotive with the help of the ironmasters at Coalbrookdale (*q.v.*) in 1802, and two years later he put the first practical railway engine into use in South Wales. He also built a steam threshing machine and was involved in various ambitious and abortive engineering projects both at home and abroad, including a proposed tunnel beneath the Thames and a railway in Costa Rica. He was always reckless and imprudent, and this great innovator in the use of steam power died penniless at Dartford in 1833, without the credit to which he was entitled. There is a statue of him in the centre of Camborne, holding a model of the Cornish engine he invented, but it is as the inventor of the steam locomotive that Trevithick's name is now most honoured.

Tring, Hertfordshire   =   MAP A

The Tring Gap is a break in the continuous ridge of the Chiltern Hills through which transport routes have been steered between Aylesbury and Hemel Hempstead, and whilst it may look fairly commonplace now, it has been the scene of engineering wonders. The Romans took their military road through the gap. When the Grand Junction Canal was constructed, the Tring Summit, where the canal was nearly 400 feet above sea level, was one of the biggest problems in its whole course. The canal remains the

highest artificial watercourse in England. Then the London and Birmingham Railway naturally opted for the same route through the Chilterns, and
the Tring Cutting was made, when men and horses moved one and a half
million tons of earth in what was reckoned to be one of the great feats of the
age. The navvies worked with picks and shovels, and one man was killed in
the course of the work. The cutting is 2½ miles long and nearly 60 feet
deep in places.

Trowbridge, Wiltshire ☆   MAP A

The prosperity created in and around the Cotswolds area by the growth of
the woollen industry in medieval times was threatened at the beginning of
the Industrial Revolution by increased mechanization, and exploitation of
the hard-worked weavers inevitably led to the strikes and riots which ran
through many troubled industries at the time. In the churchyard at
Trowbridge, which 'flourisheth by drapery' as Leland observed in the
sixteenth century, is the grave of Thomas Helliker, a nineteen-year-old
worker who was hanged at Salisbury in 1803 for taking part in a riot against
the introduction of power looms.

Trowbridge, Wiltshire □   MAP A

Several buildings survive in Trowbridge as evidence of both the cottage
and early factory textile industries of the town. Characteristic terraced
weavers' houses, on three storeys with workshop windows at the top, can be
seen in Timbrell Street, Yerbury Street, etc., and date from the late
eighteenth and early nineteenth centuries, while the mills near the town
centre – some of brick and some of stone – generally date from the
Victorian period.

Tunstall, Staffordshire △   MAP B

North-east of the town, off the Biddulph road, is the Chatterley Whitfield
Mining Museum. This colliery was among the first to produce a million
tons of coal a year, but it was closed in 1977 and is now maintained as a
museum of the industry. Exhibits include cutting machinery and winding
engines as well as the geology and technology of coal mining, and visitors
can go underground down one of the mine's several shafts; strong footwear
is required, protective helmets are provided, and infants are not admitted.
The museum is open every day except Monday. Tel: Stoke-on-Trent
813337.

Tywyn, Gwynedd   =   MAP C

The Tal-y-llyn (*q.v.*) Railway Society maintains a narrow-gauge railway museum at the Wharf Station, terminus of the line built to carry slate from the quarries below Cader Idris to the port and main railway lines here. Open daily in the summer months. Tel: Tywyn 710472.

Velindre, Dyfed   □   MAP C

At Drefach, just north of the village, is a Museum of the Woollen Industry, set up as part of the National Museum of Wales in a working mill. Visitors can see the weavers at work as well as exhibits on the local industry from medieval times. There is a collection of machinery, some dating from the eighteenth century, when the English monopoly on Welsh woollens was broken, and the women who had sat at their cottage doors with their spindles and spinning wheels began to move into factories. The mill is open daily from Monday to Friday. Tel: Velindre 370209.

Wadhurst, East Sussex   ☆   MAP A

In the churchyard, cast-iron grave slabs can be seen, which were among the products of the Wealden iron industry in the seventeenth and eighteenth centuries. 'All our yesterdays', one might say, 'light but the way to rusty death.'

Wakefield, West Yorkshire   ≈   MAP B

One or two eighteenth- and nineteenth-century warehouses remain on the quays of the Aire and Calder Navigation in this city which grew rich on the clothing trade and then on coal, and was the capital of Yorkshire's West Riding. The compartment boats which still carry coal on the canal, hauled in 'trains' by a tug, are called 'Tom Puddings'.

Ware, Hertfordshire   ▲   MAP A

Ware was an important centre of the malting trade (*see* Mistley, Essex), and several old maltings can be seen in the town, with the traditional cowled tops of their kilns and long rows of windows along the shallow floors on two storeys. These are mainly nineteenth-century buildings, all converted to other uses now, but it is instructive to stroll round the town and see what a large proportion of the working population must have been employed in the maltings at one time.

Warrington, Cheshire   +   MAP B

A transporter bridge over the Mersey was built in 1916 to link the two parts
of the Crosfield soap and chemical works. Lattice steel piers support the
semi-cantilever span of 187 feet. This was the last bridge of this kind to be
built in Britain, and it is no longer used.

Warwick, Warwickshire   ☆   MAP A

North-west of the town centre in Wallace Street are the former gasworks
which incorporated the surviving octagonal gas holders, built in 1822, with
stuccoed fronts and surmounted by louvred lanterns. The advent of gas
lighting in the nineteenth century involved housing the gas holders within
such buildings, ostensibly for additional safety, although more probably to
disguise industrial buildings in residential areas, and these buildings at
Warwick are among the few such remaining.

Washington, Tyne & Wear   △   MAP B

North-west of the town centre is a brick-built colliery engine house and
winding gear, preserved by the local authority. In the engine house is a
twin-cylinder horizontal engine built in 1888.

JAMES WATT

The great steam-engine pioneer was born at Greenock (*q.v.*) in 1736, and
at the age of twenty-one became Glasgow University's maker of mathema-
tical instruments. He did much work on canals and the improvement of
harbours before turning his attention to steam power, when he made
improvements to the engines of Newcomen (*q.v.*) and patented the 'Watt'
engine of 1769, going into partnership with the Birmingham businessman
Matthew Boulton to build engines, combining his brains with Boulton's
money. The name Boulton and Watt was soon synonymous with quality
and inventiveness, and their engines were soon replacing practically all the
Newcomen atmospheric engines installed in mines. Watt's separate con-
denser is reckoned the greatest single improvement ever made in the
technology of the steam engine, reducing the loss of power which made
Newcomen engines erratic in performance. Watt was also responsible for
the measuring of an engine's performance in terms of horsepower, having
measured the working capacity of the average horse. He defined 1
horsepower as the rate at which work is done when 33,000lb. are raised 1

foot in 1 minute. He also gave his name to the unit of electrical power. The old schoolroom fable of Watt having a brainwave when he watched a kettle boiling over is picturesque but of no consequence. As Bernard Shaw remarked of Isaac Newton's apple, we can 'take the law and leave the legend.' James Watt died in 1819, and was buried at Handsworth, Birmingham. There is a statue of him in Ratcliff Place.

JOSIAH WEDGWOOD

Wedgwood was born at Burslem (*q.v.*) in 1730, the descendant of generations of potters. He established his own factory at the age of twenty-nine, and introduced new types of pottery, such as basalt ware, Queen's ware and Jasper ware. The latter is the familiar blue stoneware with classical reliefs in white designed for Wedgwood by the sculptor John Flaxman. The cream Queen's ware got Wedgwood appointed 'Potter to Her Majesty'. In 1769 he built new factories at Etruria (*see* Hanley) with workers' cottages as well as his own mansion near the works by the side of the canal in which he was a major shareholder. He had great organizing ability, and mixed with industrial pioneers to mutual benefit. Thus, he encouraged and financed the building of the Trent and Mersey Canal by James Brindley (*q.v.*); and benefited from his friendships with Matthew Boulton, the steam engine entrepreneur, and Samuel Whitbread the brewer. He expanded and mechanized his factories under steam power, and established a production line in which skilled workers carried out their own specialized crafts on each of the products – a familiar enough method nowadays but quite revolutionary then. Thus Wedgwood laid the foundations of pottery-making on an industrial scale. He died in 1795.

West Auckland, Durham   =   MAP B

The first railway bridge of iron was built here in 1825 to carry the Stockton and Darlington Railway over the River Gaunless. It was of both cast- and wrought-iron construction. This bridge was dismantled in 1901, but has been preserved at the National Railway Museum at York (*q.v.*). The original masonry abutments remain *in situ*.

Whalley, Lancashire   =   MAP B

The town which grew up around the powerful Cistercian abbey of Whalley is now largely dominated by a brick railway viaduct built in 1850 to carry the Bolton, Blackburn, Clitheroe and West Yorks Railway across the River Calder. It has 53 arches and is nearly 700 yards long.

Whitchurch, Hampshire □   MAP A

By the Winchester road south of the town is a substantial three-storey mill
of brick on the River Test, built in 1815 as a woollen mill but later used for
silk weaving. It was originally powered by a waterwheel which remains *in
situ*. The mill stands on the site of a corn mill mentioned in Domesday
Book.

Whitchurch, South Glamorgan ≈   MAP C

The Melingriffith tinplate works in this northern suburb of Cardiff used
the water of the River Taff to drive its machinery, but ran into difficulties in
dry summers; partly because the Glamorgan Canal, which ran from
Merthyr Tydfil to Cardiff, took water from the river. Eventually a double-
beam pump engine was built, at the canal company's expense, to return
water to the canal after it had served the tin mill's purpose. It was driven by
an undershot waterwheel, and raised water on alternate actions of the
beams.

Wicken, Cambridgeshire ×   MAP A

Wicken Fen is a nature reserve owned by the National Trust, and is an area
of undrained peatland which shows what the region was like before
large-scale land reclamation took place. There is a smock mill here, built
early in the present century for drainage purposes, but re-erected here in
1956; and a small museum showing the history of the fen's evolution. It is
open to the public all the year round, and the operation of the mill is
occasionally demonstrated. Tel: Ely 720274.

Wigan, Greater Manchester ≈   MAP B

The famous 'Wigan Pier' known (or thought to be known) the world over
because of George Orwell, was actually the ironic local nickname for the
wharf on the Leeds and Liverpool Canal at Wallgate, west of the town
centre. The canal was built between 1770 and 1816, one of three canals
crossing the Pennines to link the industrial towns of Yorkshire with the
ports of Manchester and Liverpool. The Leeds and Liverpool is the only
one still navigable. It is 127 miles long and has 91 locks, 23 of them raising
the canal 200 feet in the two miles between here and Aspull, north-east of
the town.

Wigston, Leicestershire □   MAP A

West of the town centre, at Bushloe End, is a building complex comprising framework knitting workshops and master's house. This dates from the period of transition, in the second half of the nineteenth century, from the cottage knitting industry to the modern factory industry. The 'masters' in the hosiery trade were middle men who hired out the owners' stocking frames to the workers in their homes, distributed the work, and paid the men scanty wages at piece-work rates. Iniquitous practices by the masters combined with other factors – increasing mechanization and reduction in the demand for stockings when men took to wearing trousers and, not least, disastrous harvests which put the price of bread beyond the reach of the knitters – led to the Luddite riots which spread throughout the Midlands and the North. One of the answers to the problems was the setting up by the frame owners of workshops such as this one, where knitters came to the owner's premises to do their work and the masters were gradually eliminated.

Wilton, Wiltshire □   MAP A

The Royal Carpet Factory in Warminster Road is said to be the world's oldest, having been set up originally by the ninth Earl of Pembroke here in 1745. Carpets had already been woven at Wilton for some years, for by the end of the seventeenth century a Royal Charter granted the town a local monopoly, and Huguenot refugee weavers came here to work. The difference between Axminster (*q.v.*) and Wilton carpets is in the type of weave. A Wilton, which can be plain or figured, has pile yarns which are warp threads woven into the carpet. Loops are woven over sharp wires which cut the loops when the wires are lifted out, leaving a velvety pile which is then sheared. The factory is still working in the older brick buildings dating from the late eighteenth century as well as in purpose-built extensions of more recent years. It can be visited on weekday mornings. Tel: Wilton 2441.

Winchester, Hampshire ×   MAP A

The so-called City Mill, in Water Lane beside the River Itchen, was built as a corn mill in 1744. It is a brick and tile-hung building in the care of the National Trust, but leased as a Youth Hostel. There is an internal waterwheel, and much of the machinery remains *in situ*. The mill can be visited during afternoons from Tuesday to Saturday in summer, or by prior arrangement with the warden in winter. Tel: Winchester 3723.

Windsor, Berkshire   =   MAP A

The Riverside Station, designed by Sir William Tite and built in 1850, has a Royal Waiting Room built specially for Queen Victoria and designed on Tudor architectural models with bay window, turret and spirelet. The queen had first travelled by rail from Windsor to Paddington eight years earlier, when Prince Albert's verdict was, 'Not so fast next time, Mr Conductor'. The necessity for a Royal Waiting Room not five minutes from the castle seems to indicate as little confidence in trains running on time then as now. The building is now used as offices.

Windsor, Berkshire   =   MAP A

The railway bridge crossing the Thames west of the town was designed by Brunel (*q.v.*) and built in 1849. The central span is just over two hundred feet long. Brick abutments have since replaced the original cast-iron piers.

Witney, Oxfordshire   □   MAP A

Witney's association with blanket-making goes back a very long way. By Tudor times, the town was noted for weaving broadcloth, with several fulling mills spread out along the River Windrush. By the seventeenth century white blankets had become the town's principal product, and three thousand local workers were employed in carding and spinning, fulling and weaving the coarse wool of the local breed of sheep. Stone-built nineteenth-century blanket factories still dominate the town's buildings today, particularly in Mill Street and Bridge Street, and one or two older buildings survive, such as the Blanket Hall in High Street, built in 1721 by the Company of Blanket Weavers. An eighteenth-century water mill remains on the site of a fulling mill which had stood here at least as early as 1277. Even older relics of the local industry are the fourteenth-century Staple Hall in Bridge Street, and a row of almshouses near the church originally intended for the widows of blanket-makers.

Wollaton, Nottinghamshire   ☆   MAP B

Wollaton Hall, a spectacular Elizabethan mansion on the west side of Nottingham, houses the Nottingham Industrial Museum in its stable block. There are exhibits in particular on the local lace and coal-mining industries, including machinery. The hall itself took eight years to build, with stone brought from the quarries at Ancaster in Lincolnshire on horseback;

the horses doing the return journey loaded with coal from Sir Francis Willoughby's mines. The museum is open at weekends and on certain weekdays throughout the year. Tel: Nottingham 284602.

Wolverton, Buckinghamshire ≈ MAP A

The iron aqueduct carrying the Grand Union Canal across the valley of the River Ouse north of Old Wolverton was built in 1811, and is an early example of an arched suspension bridge. It replaced an earlier masonry aqueduct built by William Jessop, which itself replaced locks on both banks when the canal was first opened. But the contractor's work on the stone aqueduct was inadequate, and the aqueduct collapsed in 1808.

Woodbridge, Suffolk ✕ MAP A

Until 1957, Woodbridge had the only remaining tide mill in England still in commercial use. It was built on the estuary of the River Deben in 1793. Tidal water was impounded in a large millpond and used to drive a waterwheel of twenty foot diameter which could be undershot or breastshot according to the water level. The mill has been restored and can be seen by visitors on certain days in the summer months. Tel: Woodbridge 2048.

Woodhead, Derbyshire = MAP B

In 1838 work commenced on the Sheffield, Ashton-under-Lyne and Manchester Railway, which involved the construction under the Pennines of what would be the longest railway tunnel in the world at the time, the Woodhead Tunnel, then in Cheshire. It became one of the most notorious ventures in the history of the railways. Its original labour force of 400 navvies grew to 1,000 as work progressed. Boys and horses shifted the rubble. No accommodation was provided for the navvies apart from a few stone shelters, and they built themselves a shanty town which became a place of drunkenness and immorality, but the men had to take what little gratification they could. Standing ankle-deep in mud, they suffered disease as well as serious injury – there were blindings and amputations as well as many broken bones, and 33 lost their lives. The tunnel, which took 6 years to complete, had originally been designed to take a double track, but the enormity of the task brought last minute changes to the plans and the size of the tunnel was reduced to take a single track only. This soon proved to be a costly error. The tunnel was a bottleneck, and 18 months after the completion of the first, work began all over again on a second tunnel, parallel with the first. This one was plagued by a cholera epidemic in which 28 died, and the Woodhead tunnels were soon branded as a graveyard for railwaymen. They continued in use until 1954, when a third tunnel was completed to carry the new electrified line. You can still see the site of so much of this activity at the western end of the tunnels, though none of them is now used for passenger trains, and the two early tunnels, with their castellated masonry portals, are closed off by metal bulkheads.

Wookey Hole, Somerset □   MAP A

This village in the Mendips near Wells may seem an unlikely place to have connections with our industrial past, being more famous as the site of yawning caverns with underground rivers and a resident witch. But the river whose source is here, the Axe, has long provided the power for paper mills, one of which is still in operation in the ownership, like the caves themselves, of Madame Tussaud's. The mill dates back to early in the seventeenth century, and visitors can see the traditional method of making hand-made paper here. At one time, the chief raw materials for paper were rags, the worn-out sails of ships, and even old rope. The material was cleaned, boiled and beaten into pulp, then mixed with water to a creamy consistency. Then a frame holding fine wire mesh, called a 'deckle', was dipped into the mixture and lifted out again so that the water drained off to leave the pulp fibres behind. This was then turned on to a felt 'bed' and put under pressure. The material thus produced was dried, pressed and coated with size, and after repeating the drying and pressing process, you had one sheet of paper! The giant industry of mechanical paper-making is based on the same principles, using Esparto grass, wood pulp and other materials today. There is an important section on paper-making in London's Science Museum at Kensington (*q.v.*), but it is interesting to see the centuries-old process in operation here, and samples can be purchased. This mill was owned for a long period by the Hodgkinson family, who built the village church and school and many of the houses. The mill is open throughout the year. Tel: Wells 72243.

Worcester, Hereford & Worcester □   MAP A

The famous Royal Worcester Porcelain factory has been in business here since 1752, and some of the surviving buildings date from the latter part of the eighteenth century. It is the only porcelain factory to have been in continuous production since the early years of porcelain manufacture in

England, having been founded in Bristol in 1748 and moved here four years later under Dr John Wall and his partners. The Dyson Perrins Museum is adjacent to the factory, and contains an unrivalled collection of the firm's products over two centuries. The works can be visited by prior arrangement, and the museum is open daily except Sunday. Tel: Worcester 23221.

Workington, Cumbria △   MAP B

The Cumbrian coalfield was already being worked in the seventeenth century, and, as well as those empire-building capitalists the Lowthers, the Curwen family was one of the landowning tribes who exploited coal in this region. South of Workington town centre are the remarkable engine house and chimneys of Jane Pit, built of stone and looking like the remains of a medieval castle from a distance, with their battlemented tops. These buildings date from around 1843 and were built by Henry Curwen.

Worsborough, South Yorkshire ×   MAP B

A stone-built corn mill dating from 1625 survives beside a nineteenth-century extension at this village near Barnsley, and has been restored in full working order as a museum by the county council. The original mill was powered by a cast-iron overshot water wheel of 14 foot diameter, fed from a leat. It drove 3 pairs of millstones. The extension has 2 pairs of stones powered by an oil engine. The mill is open throughout the year from Wednesday to Sunday. Tel: Barnsley 203961.

Worsley, Greater Manchester ≈   MAP B

The Bridgewater Canal was opened in 1761 to link the Duke of Bridgewater's coal mines at Worsley with Manchester. It cut the price of coal in the city by half, and provided the impetus for the great age of canal building, as eager industrialists jumped on the bandwagon to exploit the advantages of carrying goods by water instead of packhorse and other slow and laborious means. The duke, who became known as the 'Father of Inland Navigation', employed the semi-literate genius James Brindley (q.v.) to construct the canal, and sank his personal fortune in the enterprise, which is said to have brought him at least £80,000 a year profit. Part of the canal travelled underground from the coal mines, the entrances to which are at Worsley Delph, north of the town. Drainage channels called 'soughs' were connected with the canal under ground and were made navigable at some stage to allow coal to be carried by water direct from the seams to the main waterway. Brindley's masonry aqueduct carrying the canal across the valley of the River Irwell near Manchester has been demolished, giving way to the Barton Swing Aqueduct at Eccles (*q.v.*), but it was a daring venture at the time, which fainthearts considered crazy until it proved successful and became one of the wonders of the age. Its bed was made of clay trampled down by the 'navvies' to make it watertight. The narrow boats that operated on the underground canals were called 'starvationers'.

Wortley, South Yorkshire □   MAP B

Wortley Top Forge is thought to be the only *in situ* iron works of its kind remaining in Britain, with parts dating from the eighteenth century, and it has been restored by a local voluntary society. The forge originally made iron for nails, but later specialized in railway axles until it closed down a few years before the First World War. The chief mechanical interest is a huge hammer, or helve, which was driven by a breastshot waterwheel. The original one would have been of wood, but the present one is of iron, of the type known as a 'belly helve', in which the hammer is raised by cams halfway along the shaft and allowed to fall by its own weight. There are also iron rollers dating from the eighteenth century. The forge is open on Sundays.

Wylam, Northumberland ☆   MAP B

George Stephenson (*q.v.*) was born at Wylam, in a stone cottage now in the ownership of the National Trust. The cottage itself dates from the mid-eighteenth century, and was originally a miner's cottage. It stands east of the village through the riverside country park. Only one room is open to the public, on Wednesday, Saturday and Sunday afternoons in summer.

Wylam, Northumberland =   MAP B

The village where George Stephenson (*q.v.*) was born was deeply involved in the development of colliery tramways and railways, and it was here that William Hedley's famous locomotive 'Puffing Billy' was built in 1813, following his conviction – much doubted at the time – that the friction between iron wheels and iron rails was sufficient, under the weight of a train, for a locomotive to haul wagons loaded with coal (instead of the wheels merely slipping). The railway bridge over the Tyne was built in

1876 with the platform suspended from an arch-rib construction, and was probably the earliest of its kind.

Yarm, Cleveland   =   MAP B

The railway viaduct, high above the town's rooftops, was built in 1849 to the design of Thomas Grainger, and has 43 arches of which 2 are of stone and the rest brick. The masonry arches have greater spans than the brick ones, and carry a monumental inscription as well as the river crossing. It was at Yarm where the promoters of the Stockton and Darlington Railway held their inaugural meeting.

Yarm, Cleveland   ○   MAP B

Warehouses near the medieval bridge across the River Tees are survivals from Yarm's former eminence as a port for the shipping of lead from mines on the Pennines.

York, North Yorkshire   =   MAP B

The National Railway Museum in Leeman Road is a must for all transport enthusiasts, with an unrivalled collection of railway paraphernalia and, in particular, a superb collection of steam locomotives, as well as diesel and electric ones. The L.N.E.R.'s record-breaking 'Mallard' is here, as well as a reconstruction of Stephenson's (*q.v.*) 'Rocket'. The museum provides a complete panorama of a century and a half of railway history. It is open daily throughout the year except Sunday mornings. Tel: York 21261.